Presented To:

_____

From:

_____

Date:

_____

The FUTURE of WORSHIP

The FUTURE *of* WORSHIP

PREPARING THE CHURCH FOR
A **TSUNAMI OF CHANGE**

NATHAN **BYRD**

DESTINY IMAGE® PUBLISHERS, INC.
P.O. Box 310, Shippensburg, PA 17257-0310
"Promoting Inspired Lives."

This book and all other Destiny Image, Revival Press, MercyPlace, Fresh Bread, Destiny Image Fiction, and Treasure House books are available at Christian bookstores and distributors worldwide.

For a U.S. bookstore nearest you, call 1-800-722-6774.
For more information on foreign distributors, call 717-532-3040.
Reach us on the Internet: www.destinyimage.com.

ISBN 13 TP: 978-0-7684-0290-2
ISBN 13 Ebook: 978-0-7684-8799-2

For Worldwide Distribution, Printed in the U.S.A.
1 2 3 4 5 6 7 8 / 16 15 14 13 12

DEDICATION

This book is dedicated to the "journey" that each of us must embark on if we intend to end up where God has destined for us to be.

Every once in a while there comes a change in the course of humanity that revolutionizes everything we have previously thought about an area of life; this is one of those times.

CONTENTS

FOREWORD

The *Future of Worship* is a provocative paradigm shift in how we view worship. In it, Byrd tests our beliefs and shakes us at the very core of our theological thinking concerning worship. We see him deal with the synagogue, the sanctuary, the temple, and the tabernacle. The book incites us to think beyond the traditional scope of what worship is, merely thinking that we gather and lift our hands to worship. We are taken through a study of the connection between modern Christianity and our Hebraic roots. I believe that what Byrd writes about is not only a paradigm shift, but also that it is applicable to where we are and where we are going in terms of an evolving present-day worship. This book is not for you if you are a Christian who only wants a simple blessing, if you just want to walk in the shallow end of the worship pool. Instead, if you are looking for a greater understanding of how worship is applicable to us in the twenty-first century, this book is for you.

In every age and season, when God is up to something new and fresh, He begins to release that message through His vessels. In the past, there was an emphasis on the office of the evangelist, then on the pastor and the teacher, and in recent decades a heightened awareness of the prophet and now of the apostle. As we move into a new season in the Church, the meaning of worship is going to be the prophetic picture we see changing. I believe Nathan has penned the future of worship for us. I believe that this apostolic work will provoke the Church to look at worship again—at what we do, how we do it, and why we do it. It is fresh, deep, and revelatory.

One aspect of the book that the reader will absolutely enjoy is the link between the tabernacle of Moses and the New Testament church. My mentor often speaks of the powerful association of patterns and truths in the Old and New Testaments, and Nathan Byrd builds a case for that assertion and masterfully so. Of course, there are some things that the New Testament cancels from the Old, but there are also some things to which the New Testament brings illumination. Then, too, there are things of which there is a continuation in the New Testament from the Old. Byrd does a wonderful job of illustrating each of these dynamics.

There are three major points the reader will benefit from in this book. The first is the Hebraic connection to contemporary Christianity for the contemporary Christian. The second thing is the three dimensions of worship—the Outer Court, the Inner Court, and the Most Holy Place—and their application and relevance in the New Testament Church. The third benefit is the discussion of the shekinah glory and how that glory must be the pursuit of the New Testament Church. The Church is challenged to take another look at its present worship model. For instance, many ministries are pastor or personality-centric or program-focused/directed instead of being focused on the manifest presence of the Living God. You cannot escape that we are being asked to look at the death of personality and look to the living personality of the glory of the living Christ in our worship services.

So I challenge the reader to explore this book with an open heart and mind. Yes, you may be challenged theologically and in terms of your corporate worship; however, I would caution you not to view your ministry's practices with deep criticism or disdain, but rather to engage in prayer and intercession that we would catch the powerful revelation of this three-dimensional worship Byrd expounds on and entreat others and stir them through the love of God to begin to see that there is another facet of worship in God. I believe that the truths in this book will play an integral part in the bigger picture of the next move of God in the Earth, bringing us back to the ancient highways, getting us back to the pure pattern of worship.

Bishop Victor Powell
Rhema Word International

INTRODUCTION

At The Worship Center of St. Albans, where I serve as senior pastor, we hold thematic Bible studies every three months or so. At the end of a segment of study, we take some time to digest the information that the Holy Spirit has dispersed to us and incorporate it into our regular worship experiences as well as into our lives. We have been doing this for some years now, and as I look back over the past few years of study, I have recognized a very intentional journey that the Lord has had us on.

We had just come through several studies covering such topics as: "The Hebraic Connection of our Faith," "The Ark of the Covenant," "The Ten Commandments," and "Personal Sanctification," when I stood in my office after a study had concluded and heard the Holy Spirit say specifically to write down four words. So I picked up a pen and a memo pad and wrote the words He gave me that evening, not knowing what was in store for us in days to come. I put the piece of paper in my pocket and went home.

The four words I wrote down that evening were *tabernacle, temple, synagogue,* and *sanctuary.* At the time that I wrote them down, I did not see any specific connection or understand why He told me to write them down. So I said to the Lord, "What do these words mean?"

He simply said, "I will tell you in a few days."

A few days later, while I was in the shower, the Holy Spirit started speaking emphatically about the words I had written down a few days earlier. He said to me that these are the four major eras of worship in human history. Each one represents a period of worship based upon particular circumstances in the spiritual life of Israel. Each one has major components that make worship authentic, and certain aspects of each era should have been maintained and carried forward to this day. Then He said, "I want you to research these eras and let Me show you how authentic worship should be experienced today."

From that day until now, my perspective of worship has changed almost one hundred percent. To a large degree, I feel today that my previous worship was ignorant, uninformed, and inappropriate. Having spent the past forty years walking in salvation, there have been many days that I've felt cheated by the experiences of the past that did not yield a more tangible experience with the Presence. Most of my church experiences have been superficial in that they were mostly acquainted with a "feeling" or an attempt to get something from God by my praise and worship, rather than the simple joy of being in His presence for fellowship and His pleasure. My experiences were also diminished because there was never a tangible place or symbol of His presence, just people and pulpits or stages that were the centerpiece of my attention during worship.

I will also take a moment to note here that a subsequent study on the history of the Christian Church, which took place after the "Tabernacle to Temple, Synagogue to Sanctuary" study, became more relevant and served a greater purpose in The Worship Center because we were able to see and understand when, where, and how the Church got off course, particularly as it related to the corporate worship experience. When you see how early in the life of the

Christian Church we were separated from our Hebraic roots and how the Roman influence overwhelmed the Christian culture, it is easy to see how we have arrived at our present state of confusion and disillusionment regarding our worship gatherings. Without a tangible connection to the worship that was introduced to Israel by YHWH Himself, there is no way to assemble and perform a genuine corporate worship experience today.

My analysis of what we now call worship, which will be evident throughout this book, aligns with the assessment Jesus levels upon the Samaritan woman at the well in John 4. I've read this story and heard it taught hundreds of times, and at no time have I heard anyone highlight the strong criticism that Jesus articulates in verse 22. Jesus says, *"You worship what you do not know; we know what we worship, for salvation is of the Jews."* There is no way to get around the fact that Jesus is making it clear that it is impossible to understand and participate in authentic, YHWH-pleasing worship without Hebraic components. In the absence of such, Gentile worship is futile, ignorant, and in many cases, offensive to the Father.

When I look at the evolution of worship, even in my lifetime over the past forty years, I agree with Jesus; in most cases, we have no idea what we are doing. We have gone from the priests being the only ones who understood the liturgy to black stages with colored strobe lights and smoke, from quiet non-participatory services to lively energetic services that are governed by the countdown clock. We have gone from the Lord's house to houses of worship, places of refuge to places people refuse to come to any longer. We have tried hard today, but there still seems to be no happy medium. We still have not agreed on the activity and work of the Holy Spirit in the Body of Christ. The issue of denominations and their relevancy still impacts how the world views Christianity, and without us realizing it, all of these divisions divert from the purpose of our corporate gatherings to—*"worship the Father in spirit and truth; for the Father is seeking such to worship Him"* (John 4:23).

The purpose of this book is to do just that, supply information that will equip the saints of the Most High to worship Him and give Him what He wants. There is a dramatic paradigm shift coming to the Church that will hit like the tsunami of 2004. Anyone who has been alive and aware over the past ten years can attest to dramatic shifts in the way we live and perceive the world around us. From terrorism to democracy, from climate change to health epidemics, from wealth to economic turmoil, from the presidency to the coup, from landlines to texting, things are going through dramatic and significant adjustments. Since the introduction of this new millennium, we have seen tsunami-like uprisings and shifts in countries like Thailand, Greece, Iran, Iceland, Tunisia, Yemen, Jordan, Iraq, and, most vividly, Egypt and Libya. Why should the Church miss out on this wonderful climate of unprecedented transition? Why should we continue in boredom and predictability when everything else in the world is enjoying unavoidable, unpredictable inevitability? The tsunami that is about to hit the Church will wipe out everything that was insensitive to the "peculiar signs" and did not move to higher ground.

For me, authentic worship is that higher ground. It is the "sure house" mentioned in First Samuel 2:35, where the Lord will establish what is in His heart and in His mind. As you read through this book, open your heart and prepare your mind and theology to be challenged. The challenge is to make dramatic and necessary shifts toward truth, relevance, and authenticity. Jeremiah articulates it precisely as I see it today in Jeremiah 6:16, *"Stand in the ways and see, and ask for the old paths, where the good way is, and walk in it, then you will find rest for your souls..."* Some text use the words *"ancient paths,"* suggesting that the paths are so old that it would be impossible for this generation to know that there was even a path there. The path we are looking for has to be revealed by research of ancient documents because the trees have grown in the way, and it is no longer perceptible to the modern age. This is precisely what David did when he realized he was carrying the ark the wrong way. This is what the modern Church must do if it is to accomplish authentic corporate worship in this new millennium.

When you finish reading this book, it will be impossible for you to remain complacent in your worship. It will become tangible, alive, and relevant. Whatever your occupation in the Body or your level of faith is, my goal is to introduce you to the future of worship. If you can begin to perceive where the corporate worship experience is going, you will position yourself strategically on higher ground so as to avoid the tsunami that will render many worship experiences and practices forever irrelevant.

CHAPTER 1

FOUR WORDS

When the Lord began to explain to me that the four words: *tabernacle, temple, synagogue,* and *sanctuary,* represented the four major eras of worship in the spiritual life of Israel, my first reaction was to do research on these words. My study habit in my life for quite some time has been to try not to approach a subject as if I am familiar with it already. I always attempt to do my initial research with an open heart and mind so as to gain fresh revelation from any subject, regardless of my familiarity. This made researching these words fascinating. My journey into a new understanding of worship began in a very simple word study that exploded into spirit-altering revelations.

It started with the word *tabernacle.* This term is very familiar throughout the beginning of the Old Testament. It is typically associated with the era of Moses and the children of Israel in their wilderness experience. The first time the word is used in the Bible is in Exodus 25:9. There is always great significance in the first time a word or concept is revealed in Scripture, and it should not be taken lightly. The verse here should be used in context with verse

8 to understand exactly what YWHW had in mind when He gave Moses this directive.

> *And let them make Me a sanctuary, that I may dwell among them. According to all that I show you, that is, the pattern of the tabernacle and the pattern of all its furnishings, just so you shall make it* (Exodus 25:8-9).

The first thing that must be acknowledged is that the concept of a tabernacle or sanctuary (in the Old Testament, they were synonymous) is basically identical in the eyes of the Father. The Hebrew word for tabernacle is *mishkan,* and the Hebrew word for sanctuary is *miqdash;* they obviously share very close definitions. The word for tabernacle is used to describe "a residence, dwelling place, habitation or tent," and the word for sanctuary is used to describe "a consecrated thing or place; a palace or asylum; a holy place." The root Hebrew word *qadash* means "to make, pronounce, or observe as clean; to consecrate, dedicate, hallow, prepare, proclaim, purify, or sanctify." With these two definitions, found in these two verses, which introduce the concept of the tabernacle to Moses and the children of Israel, we can get an introductory picture to what was intended at the inception of corporate worship. What the Father was prescribing for this nation was a *consecrated asylum* that would be His residence and place of habitation among them.

It's important that we don't move too fast through this period of Israel's history because there were things happening behind the scenes that set the stage for the tabernacle introduction. Firstly, we must remember that this was a re-introduction of YHWH to the nation of Israel. They had been in bondage for over ten generations, and the G-d of Israel was simply a fable or bedtime story to many in that generation. Most of them had no idea who YHWH was. When Moses came along, they were inundated with Egyptian lifestyle and worship, and YHWH had to re-introduce Himself to His own people. This is why, in the initiation of corporate worship, the

Ark of the Presence and the tabernacle had such great significance. Prior to that point, they had no reference as to what worship is and how to please the one they were worshiping. When the children of Israel were delivered from Egypt and found themselves in the wilderness at Mount Sinai, where the glory of G-d was revealed upon the mountaintop, according to Exodus 19:8, they are very willing to do whatever Moses said YHWH had spoken.

Within the context of the issuance of the Ten Commandments—or as I like to call them, the ten standards for successful living with God and people—particular things were established that set in motion what God demanded from Israel in order for them to walk in harmony with Him and each other. He began with an introduction of who He is and what He had done for them already, saying that, therefore, they had no need of any other gods. Then He established Himself as the imageless God, saying that they should never attempt to bring the graven image practice of Egypt into this relationship. Next, He commanded that His name should not be used erroneously or frivolously by Israel, thus setting a precedent for those who don't know Him to diminish the sacredness of His name. Then lastly, for the worship context, He commanded that the Sabbath day should be a day distinguished above the other six. On this day, Israel would rest and worship. Clearly the Ten Commandments are designed to eliminate any confusion or guesswork as to what YHWH expected from His people.

This sets a standard, before the tabernacle is introduced, that YHWH has preset conditions for worship and is not willing to leave those stipulations in our hands for us to figure out with our ingenuity, creativity, and personal preferences. Clearly worship has universal conditions not meant to be reinterpreted by the worshiper. Our only obligation is to follow what has been prescribed. This precedent must be followed if our present-day worship is to have any meaning from Heaven's perspective. So before the tabernacle is spoken of, a trend was established that we who are ignorant to what fellowship with the Father and worship are must be given specific instructions on how to accomplish this awesome charge.

To further set the stage for the corporate worship that is to come, YHWH gave instructions regarding the altars of sacrifice, laws of morality, and three eternal feasts, which were to be presented year after year forever (see Exod. 21–24). Modern Christianity has completely ignored these mandates and is mostly ill-equipped on how to incorporate them into today's Christianity. Due to this ignorance, we have largely chosen to omit these practices in the Church today. For example, most Christian churches completely ignore the Passover. I've often heard it confused with the Lord's Supper or communion. New Testament communion does not replace the Passover. The Passover represented a memorial for Israel. This was designed so that Israel's descendants would never forget the great deliverance from Egypt, which was wrought by the mighty hand of G-d (see Exod. 19:4). It was not a covenant celebration, as is the New Testament communion, but it is a memorial. However, as long as the Christian Church continues to function in distinct separation from its Hebraic roots, it will omit Passover, Firstfruits, and Ingathering (see Exod. 23:14-19) from its annual celebrations. As a result of these omissions, the Gentile Church has almost universally substituted Church anniversaries, pastor's anniversaries, and choir and auxiliary anniversaries to fill its calendar with special days. Not only are these things not biblical, but they are commemorating the flesh of people in the Lord's house. If worship is to be accomplished in the Lord's house, fleshly, human-made celebrations should be eliminated.

When we get to Exodus 25:8-9, Israel is given the extraordinary opportunity to enter into partnership with YHWH to build the place where the Shekinah will dwell. It is important that we embrace G-d's perspective in the invitation to *"let them make Me a sanctuary, that I may dwell among them."* G-d is giving them an opportunity to take ownership for the construction of His dwelling place so that they will always be endeared to it and connected to

Him through it. I received revelation in taking a pause over verses 8 and 9. Firstly, it says *"let them make **Me** a sanctuary,"* which makes it very clear that it is not our dwelling place, but His. How has modern Christianity dealt with this matter? We have been building houses of worship for thousands of years for the Lord's dwelling, though we only invite Him to come and visit. We build churches that basically accommodate our purposes completely. We say that they are built for the Lord, but in truth the concept behind the construction is for us. We build churches because *our* congregation size increases or the building is old or we need more office space or we need recreation space or a children's church; we build for all kinds of reasons other than to accommodate the shekinah.

I want you to take a moment and reason with me along the lines of this basic concept. If the children of Israel were about three to four million in population at the time of their deliverance—which is larger than any single congregation on Earth today—why didn't G-d have them build a three-million-seat tabernacle to accommodate the crowd? The answer is simple. It was not built to accommodate Israel; it was built to accommodate the glory of G-d.

*"Make Me a **sanctuary**..."*—make Me a consecrated place, a holy place, an asylum—*"that I may dwell among them."* It would be impossible for YHWH to simply dwell in any contaminated earthly setting. So the place of His dwelling would have to be significantly different from any other dwelling place in the Earth realm. Keep in mind that the purpose of the sanctuary/tabernacle was so that He could come down and establish His presence with Israel on a permanent basis. This in and of itself would distinguish Israel above every other nation. No other nation at any time could claim to house the actual, tangible presence of G-d. This would be an extraordinary phenomenon that is unique to Israel and could not be duplicated or competed with by any other people group.

According to this verse, there is only one purpose for building a tabernacle—so that He can dwell among us; that's it! The reason why this is so significant in our understanding of corporate worship is because this is the first time the concept of a tabernacle/sanctuary is mentioned in Scripture. It is the genesis of this idea that serves as a foundation for what we call corporate worship today. Corporate worship or worship of any kind, for that matter, was not humanly contrived; it came from G-d; therefore, it cannot be creatively enhanced or adjusted according to our desires or preferences.

To this day, I believe G-d is still in pursuit of a group of worshipers who will participate in the extraordinary partnership of building a place where He can come and stay! The Lord's house should never be called a place of His visitation; it is the place of His habitation. If you are not a visitor in your own home, why would He be a visitor in His? We are the ones who come and go from week to week, service to service. He never leaves. When we depart, He remains, and when we enter, He is already there. We should never pray the prayer, "Lord, come by here," or, "Be with us in this service, oh Lord," or, "Stop by and show Yourself strong." The question then becomes, "Why did He leave?" After all, it is His house! The fact that we pray these prayers is a clear sign that, conceptually, it is our house, and we are asking Him to show up periodically to authenticate what we have decided to do in our houses of worship. The one and only biblical reason to build a sanctuary is so that YHWH may have a habitation among His people for the purpose of worship and fellowship.

What this represents is G-d's original intent in the Garden of Eden with Adam. After the fall of humanity, we get the picture from Genesis 3:8 that Adam had fellowship with G-d on a regular basis, and it was only after sin that the fellowship was broken. The intent of Satan was really centered on breaking fellowship more than anything else. He understood that G-d enjoyed having intimate, uninhibited fellowship with His creation, just like Satan once enjoyed with G-d. Once that fellowship with humanity was broken, G-d's intent was to reestablish it based upon certain criteria and under very particular circumstances. Thus the Ten Commandments, the altars and offerings, the feasts, and the tabernacle were introduced to Israel so that the worship and fellowship could be reinstated on His terms. Israel having a tabernacle was similar to Adam having the Garden of Eden. The tabernacle represented a place where Israel was guaranteed to find the presence of the Almighty.

Next we enter into an even more controversial, yet forgotten, part of this worship process—the pattern of the tabernacle. Verse 9 makes it clear that the tabernacle architecture was not being left up to Moses or anyone else to contrive. It had already been designed and only needed construction. YHWH told Moses to make it according to all that He had showed him, that is, the pattern of the tabernacle and the pattern of all its furnishings. G-d said, *"...just so you shall make it"* (Exod. 25:9). The design of His house is not updated every century based upon our new innovations and technologies. His house is not contemporary; it is classic. It doesn't need upgrades or creative adjustments to remain relevant; it is eternal in design.

What we need to reckon with is that there is a divine pattern for the Lord's house. This pattern was clearly defined for us in Scripture. It was clearly given to Moses on the mountain, and it was his responsibility to articulate what he saw to the builders. There would be no adjustments, and G-d made that very clear in this verse. No adjustments! We'll get back to this in a moment. However, we need to focus on this simple, yet complicated, issue called the *pattern*. If we understand this, we can better understand the eternal nature of divine worship.

The pattern has to be understood in its Old Testament context and adapted into the New Testament worship experience. The continuing chapters of Exodus describe a three-compartment tabernacle design. We know it to be the Outer Court, the Inner Court (Holy Place), and the Most Holy Place (Holy of Holies). Certain activities took place in each section of the tabernacle. The Outer Court was for the slaying of the sacrifices that the people brought, the Inner Court was the place of the ministry of the priest and Levites, and the

Most Holy Place was where the shekinah (glory of the Lord) dwelt between the cherubim upon the Ark of the Covenant. By the unveiling wisdom and insight of the Holy Spirit, I understand this to be likened to three dimensions of worship. These three dimensions represent the pattern that is hidden in the Exodus 25:9 Scripture. The Outer Court is where "the worship of the sinner" takes place. The Inner Court is where "the worship of the saint" takes place. And the Most Holy Place is for "the worship of the Lord." One of the concrete things that we should understand from what YHWH instructed Moses is that this tabernacle has a prophetic pattern, and this is one of the reasons why it cannot be adjusted. Thus, we conclude that a three dimensional pattern of worship should be consistent in corporate worship eternally.

In the next chapter, I will deal with each dimension of the tabernacle as it relates to the pattern described in Scripture. However, what needs to be understood immediately is that the pattern has never and will never change. The pattern is prophetic and eternal and must be practiced today in order to experience the full measure of corporate (and personal) worship. This pattern is the actual design that Moses was to follow, as well as a spiritual pattern that defines the way to approach the Father in worship. In today's corporate worship experience, we are not informed as to how to approach G-d. We have some personally-contrived spiritual formulas, which we call liturgies, but they are typically insufficient in satisfying what G-d has already outlined as an eternal pattern for worship. This is why we so often experience hit-or-miss services in church. It is often because G-d is simply merciful to us and blesses us in spite of our ignorance, but He cannot consistently bless us lest we think that we have arrived at satisfactory worship. What He really wants is for us to seek Him until we find Him and not seek until we have come up with something creative and unique. Human creativity is killing worship right now. If we knew and understood the pattern that was given to Moses, we would experience the Presence in every corporate worship experience, all of the time. I realize that this is a bold statement, but G-d never intended for us to struggle for success in the area of worship and fellowship with Him. His desire is for us to experience Him every time we gather without difficulty.

With this in mind, I highlight briefly (and elaborate later) where the struggle originates for us today. One of the most explanative verses in the New Testament is John 4:22, where Jesus explains to the woman at the well that she does not really know who she is worshiping. What can be legitimately concluded from Jesus' statement is that, if you do not know who you are worshiping, how could you know what He wants? Jesus ends that sentence by stating emphatically that *"...salvation is of the Jews"* (John 4:22). Only in one other place in the New Testament do I see Jesus Himself make such a clear distinction as to the incapacity of Gentiles as it relates to their approach to the Father. With this in mind, I must add that, without an understanding of the Hebraic connection of Christianity to our Jewish roots, it becomes difficult to digest the revelation of what the Father is expecting of us in worship.

Throughout this book, I will make continuous commentary based on my understanding of this connection. What I understand from Romans 11, Galatians 3:6–4:7, and a myriad of other Scriptures makes it clear to me that, without an applicable understanding of our *Jewishness,* we will continue to miss and err in not only our worship, but also in our interpretation of what G-d is doing in this day and age with His Body and the world. A Hebraic worldview needs to be adapted by the Church in order for it to revamp its theology as well as its worship. This may begin within my generation with those who are less indebted to their denomination, traditions, and culture. This will begin to change the worldview and theological perspective of Christianity at large.

Next we move to the temple and its biblical usage as it relates to corporate worship. The word *temple* is defined primarily by one Hebrew word, *heykal,* which is used to describe (in the sense of capacity) "a large public building, a palace, or a temple." A more rarely used Hebrew word for temple is *bayith,* having varying applications such as "house, court, palace, place, or even prison." However, this term is often used when the phrase *house of God* is used.

In Second Samuel 7:1-17, the Hebrew word *bayith* is used to describe a "house" for our earliest context of the temple concept. Here David's concept of an earthly house (temple) is inspired by the comparison of his house to Yahweh's "tent," where the Ark of the Covenant rested. It should be noted that David's inspiration for the temple came at a time when he was resting from his enemies. This should not be taken lightly. When we are preoccupied with the battles of life, our thoughts about worship are vastly different from when we are at rest from our battles. During battles, we approach G-d based on *our needs* as it relates to the battle we are in and accomplishing victory. When we have rested from our enemies, our thoughts tend to ultimately move toward gratitude and what we can do for G-d based upon *His needs* or desires. It is at this point of rest that David's worship inclinations began to take precedent in his life, and he sought to please YHWH again.

Additionally, Israel was no longer a nomadic nation. They had their own territory, and the Mosaic tabernacle was designed for their constant movement. Now that the Ark has been recovered from the Philistines and Israel was no longer roaming from place to place, David's worshiping mindset turned toward making a permanent place for the worship of the Lord. Though Second Samuel 7 suggests that David was concerned about his legacy and the duration of his influence among Israel, YHWH guaranteed him that his house and kingdom would be established forever. However, this duration would not be dependent upon a building, but upon the Christ who was to come. Yet David's son would be honored with the privilege of building what David had envisioned and provided for.

Next, the introduction of the *synagogue* concept is very abstract. It is defined in Hebrew primarily as the "place of assembly" used by

Jewish communities, primarily for public worship and instruction, or the assembly itself. There is no mention of the synagogue edifice in the Old Testament. The New Testament Greek (*sunagoge*) bears the same meaning. The origin of the synagogue is virtually impossible to trace. However, it is believed by most scholars that synagogues became the alternative assembly for worshipers who were deprived of temple worship in Jerusalem. This means that synagogues could have developed as a result of Babylonian captivity. This makes the concept fascinating. The synagogue could and may represent the franchising of the temple at Jerusalem. The concept is purely human and has no divine connotation. In other words, God did not authorize the synagogue. Yet and still, after the temple destruction in AD 70, the synagogue became premier to Jewish life and served as the place where the Law of Moses and Jewish manners, customs, and beliefs were interpreted. In the long-run, it would serve a great purpose in preparation for modern Christianity.

The goal of the tabernacle and temple were to provide a place for the shekinah to dwell. This presence, as I like to refer to the glory of G-d, was tangibly present between the cherubim above the Ark of the Covenant. As Israel grew and spread out in a vast geographical area around Israel, it became impossible for each family to come to temple worship on a weekly basis; thus, the synagogue served the purpose of providing a place for prayer, Scripture reading, and instruction by a local rabbi. This is why, in the New Testament, we have so many stories of people journeying to Jerusalem for the main feasts of Israel. This represented the time when everyone felt a mandate to worship "at the temple," where the tangible presence of the Lord dwelt. He was not manifest in the synagogue in this way. And the fact of the matter was that there was no Ark in the synagogue.

This gives insight to where our Gentile system of local churches comes from. In essence they are like synagogues—places designed for prayer, Scripture reading, instruction, and some form of corporate worship. The pattern or design would naturally be more casual and not be reminiscent of the three dimension tabernacle pattern.

Jesus did not ignore the synagogue, but used it for teaching, preaching, and healing. However, His ministry constantly undermined what had been happening in those synagogues. He got overwhelming crowds; He did not teach like the Pharisees; He saw manifestations when He taught; and he asserted what should be happening in these synagogues if they had the right leadership. The indictments that Jesus levied on the synagogue so often match the indictments on the Christian Church experience because the two settings mimic each other.

The leadership often referred to the synagogues as "theirs," which is similar to what we see today. This creates a sense of separation or denomination. They had strong hierarchy and structure. Jairus was referred to as a "ruler" of the synagogue in Mark 5:22. We find the same types of hierarchies in churches today. According to Luke 13:10-17, they seem to misinterpret their responsibilities as it related to providing ministry to broken, hurting, or sick people. Jesus considered the ruler a controller and a hypocrite. We see that today in many churches everywhere—people who are in positions of power to control the church and at the same time exhibit hypocrisy in their own lives. In John 9:22, we see that the leadership would put you out of the synagogue if you disagreed with them; this is still true today in most controlling ministries. Matthew 10:17 makes it clear that the leadership ruled with an iron thumb. They would persecute people by trial and scourging by the "council" in the synagogue. This practice is still very active and justified in the Church today.

They were also places of unchecked bad theology. Two of many examples are found in Matthew 3:7-9 and John 8:37-59, where the Jews relied solely on the connection to father Abraham as their security for salvation rather than doing the work of their heavenly Father. Jesus upbraided them for their flawed thinking and interpretation of Scripture. Some of the theology that we hear of today is very simply the result of a tolerance worldview that has arrested the world and is now influencing the Church. We are so intimidated and afraid to interpret Scripture accurately because we fear what society will say about such "dogmatic" views about the way in which we are to live. This is exactly the reason why our theology doesn't hold up under great scrutiny. Even the forefathers of the Church seem to have had more backbone than we in this modern era. However, truth and standards will win in the long run.

Lastly, the synagogue turned into a place of pride and showmanship, according to Matthew 6:2,5; 23:1-6, 23-27. Jesus reprimanded the scribes and Pharisees for these actions that became so distractive to the synagogue that the practice of the prayer, the reading of the Scriptures, and the instruction retained no value. Our churches look just like this, and this is the main reason why some people choose to worship at home or have a "coffee shop" fellowship. I could go further with the improprieties of the synagogue, but I'm sure these examples make clear how the modern Church and the synagogue share faults and failures.

Obviously, the synagogue system may have had good intentions at the outset, but it turned into a place of fear and control in the long run, just as has many local assemblies today. This system failed primarily because it lacked the divine mandate, but also because it became a place centered on the preeminence of an individual leader (or leaders) and not the preeminence of the Presence.

Finally, we must introduce and discuss the sanctuary era of worship, of which we are partaking presently. *Sanctuary,* as previously mentioned, is defined by the Hebrew word *miqdash,* meaning "a consecrated thing or place; a palace or asylum; holy place." The root Hebrew word *qadash* means "to make, pronounce, or observe as clean; to consecrate, dedicate, hallow, prepare, proclaim, purify, or sanctify." Exodus 15:17 is the first Old Testament reference using the word for sanctuary (*The Song of Moses*). Moses envisioned, after the exodus from Egypt, that YHWH would bring His people to a safe and secure place. He described it as best he could as an asylum or "a place of Your own dwelling." In other words, this great and mighty deliverance was not a random, abstract work of the Lord. It had a very definitive purpose, and that was to bring the people out to the wilderness so that they could "sacrifice" or worship the Lord, as described in Exodus 3:18. If the purpose of the deliverance was worship, then YHWH would provide a place for that worship, and it would have to be a place that He established and indwelt.

According to Leviticus 19:30, the sanctuary was a place for G-d to be revered. In this verse, the Hebrew word *yare* is used to describe "to fear, revere, or frighten." In the Old Testament there was a great fear regarding entering and serving in the Presence. The priests and Levites understood that they should never take for granted their sin and imperfection when standing before a holy and awesome G-d. There was extensive preparation spiritually and naturally that preceded their daily service. This kind of reverential fear is no longer found in our worship services. This tragic disregard for the Lord's house is the reason why our churches are now referred to as houses of worship. The fear in Leviticus is directly related to being in the tangible presence of the Lord, and there is no one in Scripture who approached the Presence without fear and reverence. Revelation 1:17 says that John *"fell at His feet as dead";* the power and awe of the experience of being in the same space as Jesus Christ is beyond words. Do we take the Lord's sanctuary lightly? I would say we do. There needs to be a greater reverence for the sanctuary of the Lord and the presence of G-d.

In contrast, Leviticus 26:2 uses the Hebrew word *shachah* to describe reverence, meaning "to depress, prostrate, or bow (self) down in reflection to royalty or as a sign of worship." Clearly, this is not the depiction we find in most worship today. It is heartbreaking to me to see churchgoers miss the significance of this holy place of worship and exhibit such defiance to the purpose of the environment. I often wonder why anyone would subject themselves to such an environment if they have no intentions of submitting to the spirit of worship. Periodically, I get a strong desire to protect the atmosphere by encouraging them to worship or leave. I know that seems extreme. Yet in Exodus, Moses and the Levites were instructed not to let any strangers into the tabernacle at all.

According to Psalm 63:2, the sanctuary should be a place where we desire to see the power and glory of G-d on display. The psalmist says that he has "looked for" the Lord in His sanctuary. This is an expression of the desire, thirst, and longing that typically precede manifestation. There must be an *expectation* and *anticipation* before we see the move of G-d in His sanctuary. There must be intention on our part and focus on Him; otherwise, we tend to give the glory to the wrong person. At The Worship Center (TWC), where I am senior pastor, we once spent almost half a year just focused on those two words every time we came into the sanctuary. We would remind ourselves that we expected G-d to do something while we were gathered. We also would praise and worship in anticipation of a supernatural manifestation. Entering the sanctuary to worship with this attitude changed everything about the experience. We would not be in a rush to do the next thing. We lingered in worship; we became more open to the spontaneity of the Spirit. It was and remains our approach to every worship experience. I believe the Father is seeking such to worship Him in this way, and He gets excited and moves quickly to inhabit the praises of His people. The manifestations that have come as a result are too numerous to mention, and we believe the best is yet to come.

Scripturally, the sanctuary has always been a place of praise and celebration of the Lord. Though we have decided it is okay to praise and celebrate everybody in His house, it was never so. Psalm 134:2 makes it clear that the sanctuary is the place where we bless and celebrate the Lord for what He has done. As a part of this celebration, our hands should be lifted, our voices should be raised, and our posture and presentation should be reminiscent of the greatness of our G-d. What has happened to this reverence for the Lord's house in recent years? We have based what we call worship upon cultural influences and denominational mandates, and in order to do this, you must ignore Scripture.

Scripturally, the sanctuary has been a place of profound understanding. In Psalm 73:1-17, there is a wonderful portrayal of the dilemmas that face the saints as we look at the lives of the rebellious. We all periodically wonder about how they can live so contrary to the will of G-d and seem to prosper. The psalmist almost seems to be pained by all that he sees as opposed to what the righteous are experiencing. However, when he gets down to verses 16 and 17, the resolve comes as a result of his sanctuary experience. Going to the sanctuary should answer life's difficult dilemmas and set the heart at ease, not create greater difficulty of understanding. We should not hear a message and walk away bewildered. We should get profound answers that give us peace and help us to comprehend the end or the bigger picture. We should experience clarity and resolution after we have worshiped. The Holy Spirit must have free course to minister words of healing, strength, and comfort to the saints when they have given their all in worship. In essence, we must leave different from the way we entered. That is the end result of having been in the sanctuary. When reality rules the psyche, there is a remedy for the righteous: the sanctuary.

In understanding the issue of the Lord's sanctuary as it relates to New Testament worship and the era we now exist in, I must introduce some additional information about the sanctuary that will serve as a foundation for the framework of what this worship looks like.

The reason why modern worship comes up short has much to do with our understanding of the pattern of the Mosaic tabernacle as well as the true tabernacle that is described in Hebrews 8:1-2. I stated earlier that, according to Exodus 25:9, there is a pattern that was not only applicable in the Mosaic tabernacle, but is prophetic and genuine for today's worship blueprint. In fact, this pattern is unchanging, primarily because when YHWH introduces it to Moses, He states emphatically that it must not be adjusted or changed one iota.

This intrigued me during my initial research because I wanted to know why G-d was so specific and definitive about the "pattern" of this worship facility. Why was it so important not to change or amend anything from the design that was given to him on the mountain? Was it just G-d being G-d, or was there some other specific reasoning behind this mandate. As it turns out, this is where the revelation of the tabernacle/sanctuary comes alive. Apparently, the writer of Hebrews (by the Holy Spirit's inspiration) wanted us to know *where* our High Priest is seated. This "where" is not figurative, but literal, since Christ is real and alive. He describes the location as a seat at the right hand of the throne of the Majesty *"in the heavens"* (Heb. 8:1). So we have a specific location, and it is not in any way earthly.

Hebrews 8:2 then states that He is a Minister of *"the sanctuary and of the true tabernacle,"* which the Lord erected and not people. Now this is fascinating if you keep the context literal. The writer is very clear that the location of the Christ is in a literal sanctuary, and this sanctuary is in fact the true tabernacle because it is the original one that was designed and erected by YHWH Himself. What must be understood here is that the Greek word (*hagion*) in context is interpreted as "a sacred holy place"; in fact, it suggests this is the holiest place of all places in all the creative works of the Creator. There is no place holier than this place. This place was not only pitched (*penumi*) by YHWH, but the design has *no human origin*.

We are dealing with something that is beyond human capacity and creativity. The connection to the Exodus 25:9 mandate is found right here in Hebrews 8:5, where it states that the Mosaic tabernacle and its design served as an earthly "copy and shadow" of what already existed in the heavens. This is the reason why Moses could not adjust what was divinely instructed on the mountain. He had to make it according to the "pattern" because all he was doing was making a copy of what already existed in Heaven, where the Father and the Son presently dwelled in all splendor and glory.

If you have digested that, you now have a foundation upon which you can begin to understand the prescription for worship in the New Testament Church experience. There is one prophetic pattern that must be used if G-d, by His Presence, will come down to the Earth realm and stay for corporate fellowship; under any other circumstances, He will only visit us. What we must reckon with is that our sanctuaries do not follow the divine pattern naturally or spiritually, and in both cases, it becomes counterproductive to the sustained Presence. I will elaborate more on this particular facet of worship in the chapter on real sanctuary worship.

The earthly worship service is only a copy or example of the unseen (mysterious) sanctuary worship in glory. What we see in our worship services is a gross misrepresentation of such a glorious heavenly experience. There is a spiritual pattern that must be followed in order to draw near to the Presence. If this protocol is not understood or is ignored, then we have missed the point of our worship. Most worship services are centered upon the parishioners feeling good when it is completed, but the worship should be centered upon YHWH being satisfied when it is done. Once the objective of worship is shifted away from us and back to making the Father happy, then we will begin do things differently in our sanctuaries. This radical approach to worship is going to revolutionize the Church and cause the glory of God to return to the sanctuary. When we return to the protocol of the Outer Court, Inner Court, and Most Holy Place, then G-d is compelled to be in the midst of His people. Returning to the original purpose for the sanctuary (*"so that I may dwell among them"*) will cause us to experience the tangible and, in many cases, visible Presence of the Lord.

Imagine for a moment that you leave your house and go on a long journey to a foreign land. You arrive, and your host picks you up from the airport and takes you to his house, where you will be lodging for a month. When you get there, you notice that the yard and exterior of the house have a strange resemblance to your house back home. As you get closer, you find that the shape, structure, and size are the same as your house. Then you enter, and as you enter beyond the door, you see that the main floor set-up is exactly the same as your home. You are feeling strange now. Then you go upstairs to the guest room, you discover that it is exactly as yours is at home. Suddenly, the feeling that comes over you is that you feel like you are at home. In fact, you are so comfortable that you don't even feel the need to return to your home. Well, the concept is exactly the same with G-d. In order for Him to come down to Earth and stay, He must feel at home. Everything about His dwelling place on Earth must match His dwelling place in Heaven if He is to come and feel comfortable enough to stay. Moses' only obligation was to make it exactly the same so that when He descended from glory there would be no difference in His dwelling place.

G-d is not impressed with the size or the user-friendly state-of-the-art functionality of the church building. If it does not make Him feel at home, He's only going to visit from time to time. As the Church weighs its relevancy and influence in the Earth today, it must face the reality that the primary reason for our existence is to be His praise in the Earth. The single most important thing a church can do is provide an environment where the Lord is comfortable and an atmosphere of worship for those who enter its gates. If it does not provide that, why does it exist? We must return to original intent and serve the purpose for which we have been left on the Earth. We must do whatever it takes and risk the ridicule of our peers so that we can accomplish the will of G-d.

These four words which represent the eras of worship throughout the history of humankind are the backdrop of all that will be discussed in this book. These initial definitions serve as a platform upon which we can build a tangible and relevant theory of what worship should look like today. When the Lord originally gave me these four words, He said that in each era of worship there are things to be maintained and things that are no longer applicable. Part of my instruction was to search the Scriptures and, by the help of the Holy Spirit, decipher what should still be practiced to authenticate worship today. Each era contains ingredients that should be carried forward, and if they are practiced today, we should experience the Presence without fail.

As a final thought on this process of discovery, the Lord gave me Jeremiah 6:16. It says,

> *Stand in the ways and see, and ask for the old* [ancient]
> *paths, where the good way is, and walk in it; then you will*
> *find rest for your souls....*

One version says, *"Stand at the crossroads and look"* (NIV). For me, this represents an opportunity for the Church to contemplate and make a good decision as to its direction and destiny. However, upon further research and study, I found that the text was suggesting something more. When I first read and understood that I was standing at a crossroads, I thought it meant that I should be making a decision based on two choices ahead of me. But the Holy Spirit revealed that, in the place where the Church stands today, there are visible roads of recent history and popular opinion ahead of us. But the road that the Lord has for us to walk on is ancient. It is not visible to the naked eye, and in fact recent history and popular opinion shed no light on this particular road. This road is so old that it is presently indistinguishable to the eye. It is indeed ancient. Great big trees have now grown in the path, and this generation is completely unaware that a road even existed in this area. So none of the roads we are looking at represent the true choices of today. The only way to

discover what the Lord is referring to is to go back to ancient litera-
ture (the Bible) and revisit its mysteries.

My search was for something I had not known or experienced.
My search had no predetermined markers. My search would uncover
information that neither this generation nor several generations
before had ever come to discover. This would be the only way I
would arrive at a fresh truth. My search would also put a mantle and
a mandate on my life to cut down the colossal pine trees of theological dogma so that the "good way" of revelatory relevance could again
be tread on. So I stood at the crossroads and found that neither exist-
ing path was sufficient to satisfy the desire of Adonai. As a result, I
have taken the risk to forge ahead down a road of ancient truth to see
if we have forsaken some valuable revelation along the way. Hopefully, what has been discovered will not only change the life of the
individual saint, but also the Church of the Living G-d universally.

CHAPTER 2

MULTI-DIMENSIONAL WORSHIP

In the previous chapter, I stated that the tabernacle consists of a particular pattern or design. This pattern is crucial in our understanding of corporate worship. In Exodus 29:42-46, there is a description of what would take place on a continual basis within the tabernacle. YHWH says that He will meet and speak with the children of Israel there at the tabernacle on a consistent basis. This means that the primary purpose of the tabernacle was as a meeting place. This meeting place is not for us to meet with ourselves obviously. It is for us to meet with YHWH; this is an essential of the tabernacle. Additionally, the sons of Aaron would minister to the Lord there, and YHWH would confirm His relationship and commitment to His people. The question becomes, "How does this design serve to accomplish this task continually, and is it still relevant today?"

I make the assumption that there is no dispute as to the purpose of the tabernacle (meeting place) then and now. YHWH still desires to meet with us on a consistent basis, and He still desires to confirm His relationship with His people. That being established, we begin by taking a closer look at each dimension of the Mosaic tabernacle because it represents YHWH's original intent and the origination of corporate worship. Our goal is to extract from the ancient what is still relevant today and to understand how to incorporate it into our New Testament or modern corporate worship experiences.

Now let's further describe what we are dealing with in each dimension. The Outer Court, or first dimension of worship, is the place where the *guilty* brought an *honest* sacrifice to the Lord. The Outer Court deals with the (sinful) flesh of humanity. This is the reason why I call this dimension "the worship of the sinner." The first step in the corporate worship is designed for personal acknowledgment of sin and guilt, and in this case, the animal sacrifice represented repentance and asking for forgiveness. This dimension of worship is significant and necessary for us to begin our approach of the Almighty. There should be no dispute that this step is still necessary in the life of the New Testament Church today. Unfortunately, most worship experiences today only take us to this point. Most don't take you much farther than the acknowledgment of sin and the need for repentance. This is an imperative; however, if the ministry only brings you to this point, it will, in the long-term, be deficient. There are two more dimensions that you the worshiper are not being exposed to.

We can see a similar concern in Acts 19 when Paul meets with some disciples in Ephesus. After a few days of observation, He asked them, "Have you received the Holy Spirit since you believed?" According to their response, they had not even heard of the Holy Spirit. Evidently, the ministry that had introduced them to salvation had left them at the baptism of John to repentance and gave them nothing more. This is where many ministries and denominations have dropped Christians off, and those same Christians have become disillusioned with their faith. In the same context as Paul in Acts 19, what I have noticed is that most worship leaders and pastors are not aware of another dimension of worship. This is understandable because, just as in the case of the disciples at Ephesus, whoever introduced them to the faith did not have any further revelation themselves.

It is important to note that if you are open to deeper and more involved levels of understanding regarding worship, you are about to be introduced to dimensions that will transform your worship forever. This will start you on a journey of untold and unsearchable plateaus of praise, thanksgiving, singing, and asylum with G-d. If we can acknowledge that the worship most Christians experience today is equivalent to the Outer Court of worship, then we must pursue with humility and anticipation the next comparative dimensions of worship. Based upon our understanding of the Mosaic tabernacle (YHWH's original intent for earthly worship), we must investigate at least two more dimensions of corporate worship.

The second dimension of worship is the Inner Court or the Holy Place. This is the place I refer to as "the worship of the saints," and it deals with the souls of people. In Moses' day, it was the place of priestly preparation. This dimension is designed to minister to the Church. All of the furniture and fixtures typify the Church, such as the table, the candlestick, and the showbread. The table represents a place of learning or instruction. The candlestick represents illumination or revelation, and the showbread represents divine nourishment or sustenance. It is the place for instruction, obedience, and development of the Body of Christ. It is impossible to enter the Most Holy Place without going through a season in the Inner Court. It represents a place of maturity and seasoning. This is where we are prepared for worship, praise, and intercession.

What should happen each week in the local church is that the teaching, preaching, and ministry activities should be preparing the individual worshipers to enter the Most Holy Place on their own, in their own time. Most ministries are not aware of this reality, and as result, if they bring the worshiper to the Most Holy Place, it is accidental, unexpected, and almost shocking. I say that to capture what happens in some churches when they have a phenomenal worship service. Sometimes people leave the sanctuary saying, "The Lord sure stopped by today," or, "What a move of G-d that was today," almost as if they didn't know how it happened, what precipitated it, or how to experience it again. In this case, the ministry only leaves you wanting more and not knowing how to accommodate that desire. The next week you come to church with a sense of expectation, only to be disappointed when the service simply follows the printed program or typical format of worship. This is spiritually unhealthy.

If the Church doesn't know how to achieve Most Holy Place worship each and every Sabbath, it will project an image of an inconsistent idiosyncratic G-d who is completely illusive and unpredictable in regard to His presence. Additionally, if the ministry doesn't go beyond the Holy Place (Inner Court), it will always depend upon a priest (pastor) for all of its spiritual fortitude. It will create a codependent relationship which eventually ends up as an exploited relationship. I will elaborate on some of these matters in this dimension further in the coming chapters.

If the pattern or worship has not been defined, then each worship service takes on its own characteristics based upon the varying banners that we gather under—for example, Sunday morning worship, anniversary, concert, prayer meeting, or Bible study. What the Church really needs is to have an understanding of why we have gathered and to become committed to that purpose every time there is a corporate worship experience. This way the tone is set and the Father has free course to manifest His presence any way He desires; our job is simply to remain open to His direction for that experience. Additionally, it takes the pressure off of the pastor or choir or worship leaders to "perform" for the congregation. Once this is established, they can take the posture of Aaron and his sons and simply "minister to the Lord."

Finally, there is the Most Holy Place. This is the third dimension of worship. I call it the place of "the worship of the Lord," and it deals with the spirits of people. This is the place where the tangible presence of the Lord dwells between the cherubim of the Ark of the Covenant. The Most Holy Place is an awesome place to enter into. It is the ultimate experience in worship. It is reaching back to the days of Adam, when he met G-d in the cool of the day; it is a face-to-face experience with no barriers and no hindrances. It is reminiscent of Enoch walking with G-d.

In Moses' day, the priest went in once a year for the atonement of the sins of the nation of Israel. However, because of the blood of Christ—according to Hebrews 10:18—we have been given unprecedented access to this place (dimension) of worship. It is the ultimate goal and end of all worship. It is the place of the glory (shekinah) of G-d. It is also the place where all attention is on YHWH. The priest always went in alone, and there was no other influence and nothing in this dimension to distract him. In our worship services today, we know that we do not enter the Most Holy Place because we are always being distracted by human beings. In the Most Holy Place, there was no human influence; it was just the priest and the Presence. This is where all corporate worship should take us. Corporate worship should always end up in a place where no one has to say or do anything to encourage or embellish the worship. The worshipers are in the face of YHWH, and He Himself inspires the worship. This is the dimension of "the worship of the Lord!"

In the Most Holy Place, there are some significant furnishings that we are aware of, the most important of which is the Ark of the Covenant. It consists of the tablets on which the Ten Commandments were written, the mercy seat, and the cherubim that face each other. YHWH says, at least eight times, beginning in Exodus 25:22, that He will dwell and speak from between the cherubim. I understand this to mean that the Most Holy Place contains the *tangible* Presence as manifest in the Earth realm. G-d makes it very clear to Moses and thus to Israel that they will not have to search for Him or wonder where He is; He is giving them His actual earthy location. This is a monumental revelation as it relates to what we have known and experienced as corporate today. This removes the guesswork from where G-d is and how to access His presence.

I should also note that the Most Holy Place is a fearful place in that the priest went in once a year and served in reverential fear before the Presence. It has been said that his garment would have bells sewn onto the hem and their jingling would signify that he was still alive and trembling in the Presence. Also a rope was possibly tied to his leg so that if He expired in the Presence, due to inappropriate preparation or sin, no one would need to go in to get him; they would simply drag him out by the rope.

When the priest went into the Most Holy Place to minister before the tangible presence of the Lord, there was no one and nothing else in that dimension. All of his attention was on the glory and presence of the Lord. When he looked upon the ark, each component of the ark spoke to his life and the life of Israel. Firstly, it was overlaid in gold. This signifies the glorious splendor and glamour of our G-d. Secondly, the priest would see the Ten Commandments, which were the instructions of how to live a pleasing and satisfactory life with the G-d of Heaven and with fellow people on Earth. Of course, seeing the Commandments was convicting because he was found wanting in regard to these standards. Thirdly, he also saw the mercy seat, which was comforting because, in spite of his shortfalls, G-d would have mercy on him. And then lastly, the cherubim would remind him of the praise and worship he was obligated to offer before the Father for His goodness, His mercy, and His love demonstrated to the children of Israel.

This is what we should be experiencing every single time we gather for corporate worship. After we have acknowledged our sin in the Outer Court, we enter into the Inner Court, or the Holy Place, so that we can receive instruction and revelation about the Father. After receiving this instruction, we should find ourselves prepared to move on our own (the blood of Christ having made the way) into the Most Holy Place. Once the corporate worship experience prepares you for this dimension, you are obligated to go in and worship before the face of G-d without human influence. Once this happens, we become accountable to G-d and not to people to fulfill what He has spoken to us while we were in that dimension. This matures the saints and causes development beyond that of a human discipline. Most Holy Place worship is reminiscent of the personal and intimate fellowship of G-d and Adam. This was and will always be what G-d is after with His creation: personal intimate fellowship.

In most cases, the worship we experience today is designed to limit our access to either the Outer Court or the Holy Place. You can tell if you are in an Outer Court worship experience because all you feel is a need to repent or you are reminded of your weaknesses or you are reminded of your flesh and its problems. Everything from the music to the message keeps you struggling in the flesh realm, and you never feel like you can get any closer to G-d or have any greater access to G-d outside of the priest who laid your sacrifice on the altar and consequently instructed you by influence not to forget to come back next week and do it again. A corporate worship experience like this will limit you from accessing the Holy Place.

Similarly, you can be in a church that limits you to the Holy Place. Many of our churches have moved to this level, where you receive good instruction and revelation as to how to live the Christian life successfully. This experience deals with the souls of people; their minds and hearts are challenged to do better and be better. These ministries have conferences, trainings, and strategies to help people become better Christians. However, they often hinder you from entering into the Most Holy Place because, if you do, they fear that you won't need them like you needed them previously. They also fear that they will not be as great and amazing in your eyes if you begin to see the Father face-to-face on your own. As long as you only see the Father through them, they can exploit and control your relationship with the ministry and keep you in submission. This was not and will never be the plan of the Father since He clearly states in Exodus 19:6 that we would be a *"kingdom of priests."* This means that His desire is for the corporate assembly to have access to His Presence in a common and universal way. This type of intimacy allows for everyone to be an advocate and an ambassador for the kingdom in their sphere of influence. So nowadays our advanced ministries do wonderful teaching and development of the soul, but typically leave us short of being transformed by personal and pure access to the Father.

Three-dimensional worship is not understood because Gentile worship goes back so far in history that very few have taken the time to re-examine why we worship the way we do. It has basically been accepted that the worship we experience today has always been and is by that measure correct. From century to century, we have simply accepted the practices of the previous generation as legitimate and authentic. We have only ventured to update the church experience based upon technological modernization, greater social suitability, or as of late, marketing strategies. Very few, if any, of our updates and adjustments are based on revelation from the Word of G-d. A revelatory examination of Scripture would expose the genuine purpose of worship and how to accomplish it in every era of human existence.

What needs to be considered is the pattern that is described in Old Testament Scripture and its spiritual significance in today's corporate worship. Often when I share these concepts with leaders of the contemporary Church, they misinterpret my commentary as inappropriate or inaccurate for the New Testament Church because of the blood of Jesus. However, it is for that very reason that I question why we worship the way we do today. Today's worship, whether Catholic or Protestant, still seems to be restricted based upon a human mediator. In the Catholic Church, that mediator is the priest or ultimately the pope. In the Protestant Church, it is subliminally the pastor, bishop, or elders. In both cases, the suggestion based upon the propagated theology is that you need a spiritual authority to advocate or represent you to the Father, thus diminishing the significance of the blood of Christ.

What I'm advocating is that, because of Christ, we have direct access to the Father (in the Most Holy Place), and with that access we have an obligation to be a community of priests among the lost. If the assumption remains that only a few specially-qualified people have this special access, then the mission of the kingdom of God is minimized by the small representation of prepared saints. This could not possibly be the paradigm of ministry Jesus promoted during His earthly ministry. Still, if the concept of corporate worship remains that the majority of those who attend are only there to observe and benefit from the gifting of a few leaders who function from an extraordinary spiritual capacity, we will never see the need for open access to the Most Holy Place.

This type of corporate worship has only produced an impotent, ill-equipped, emotional, and needy group of congregants who can barely survive from Sunday to Sunday—thus setting up a perfect scenario for exploitation of the sincere seeker. These church-goers possess very little knowledge, confidence, faith, prayer power, and spiritual fortitude to accomplish anything for the sake of the kingdom. This is the primary reason why worship in the third dimension is so necessary. Corporate worship that goes beyond the pulpit personality, the emotion or inspiration of a song, and the protocol of the liturgy is what people need to walk in a new dimension of kingdom power and authority. In my estimation, it is an essential part of the preparation for the Body of Christ to be duly suited as a bride for her bridegroom.

This is the inevitable change that is coming to the structure and arrangement of this present Church system. It reminds me of the way the high priest and rulers of the synagogue felt when Jesus came along and spoke things to the community that exposed their inauthenticity and their ineffectiveness. In that case and in ours today, it is important to remember that the work of Christ was not centered on the endorsement of a person or a group that previously existed; it was centered on the establishment of the kingdom of G-d in the Earth realm. Jesus spent His time recruiting, discipling, and empowering citizens for His kingdom. The time has come to disregard the opinions of our constituents and to take a stand for Christ and His kingdom agenda.

With this in mind, I would like to walk you through what makes this third-dimension worship so transformational and tangible for me.

In all of my Christian experience, the corporate worship has always been directed toward a feeling of ecstasy or a "spiritual high," which is provided by a presumed spiritual leader—a pastor, preacher, or singer. The person providing this spiritual service has always been the focus of my attention and inspiration. Though I knew G-d was involved in the experience, it was always very closely associated with a human being. This is the conceptual understanding of most people who walk into a corporate organized worship experience. What makes this third dimension understanding of worship so powerful is that it is completely separate and distinct from the service provided by the spiritual leader. It makes the Presence of YHWH paramount, and it gives tangible expression to the location of the Presence. It makes it very clear where you can find the Presence in the corporate setting, and it sets precedence for how to enter in and enjoy the Presence. It also puts the onus on the participant for authentic worship and not just the spiritual leader. It provides a new standard for the accountability of the worshiper.

In the third dimension, one must remember that it deals exclusively with the spirits of people and not their flesh. So there is nothing that can be done in the flesh that will be viewed as more pleasing or satisfactory to G-d. What this does is release the saints from any type of unnecessary emotion or physical demonstration, which we often see in our worship today. It also releases the saints from thinking that there is a spiritual activity that they can do in the natural to please G-d more than someone else. The spirits of people become intimate with the Spirit of G-d, and there is an honest, truthful fellowship, similar to that of Adam and G-d before the fall.

In the Most Holy Place, all of the attention is on YHWH. So again, there is no human distraction in this dimension. No one directs you, no one hinders you, no one says what you can and cannot do; it is a pure and undefiled worship of the Almighty. The third dimension of worship also creates an unusual anticipation for what is to come. Since the blood of Jesus has been shed, the veil between the Holy Place and the Most Holy Place has been rent in two; this transition creates anticipation like we've never seen before in worship. Unlike in the Mosaic experience, you can see into the next dimension. You can see from the Holy Place where you are going and anticipate before you get there. This changes the entire context of the Holy Place. Today we view or function as if the Holy Place is the ultimate end of worship. But now, with this dimension revealed and exposed, we are able to understand that there is another level of worship to be achieved, and we begin to anticipate it before we get there. Imagine worshiping in the Holy Place and seeing the Ark of the Covenant and the Presence just a short distance away. It makes the second dimension a dimension of serious preparation. It changes it from a place where we just shout and dance and feel good to a place where we value the instruction that is being given because we see its importance as it relates to our ability to enter the next dimension with boldness and confidence. This would remove the jokes and foolishness we so often see in churches that grieve the Holy Spirit and the Father. It also puts a greater demand upon the spiritual leaders to be endowed with spiritual wisdom and revelation so that they may adequately supply the saints with what they need to successfully enter before the Presence without shame or doubt.

Once the Church walks into this revelation of worship, everything about our corporate worship experience will change. Now the saint will be able to comprehend what Jesus has provided for us in worship and fellowship; however, the access will only be restricted by what's going on within the believer and not without. If there is a lack of faith in the finished work of Christ or a lack of confidence in the Holy Spirit's direction, it will show up when you enter into this dimension. Just as the priest entered with reverential fear, so the saint must enter with the same level of respect for the Presence. The Presence of the Almighty cannot be taken lightly or casually. This tangible connection to the Presence is what the Church needs today to restore holiness, fear, and respect to the body of believers. It is the very thing that is missing from our corporate worship experiences today. I believe that if leaders had to minister just a few feet in front of the tangible, visible Presence of G-d, they would certainly practice a different behavior in and away from the sanctuary.

The third dimension of worship allows us to enter into the shekinah glory and receive revelation as if we were seated in heavenly places with Christ Jesus. In order for the Church to reclaim a place of prominence and distinction among other religions, we must have access to information that the world cannot attain. Spending time in the shekinah will put us in a place of receiving the type of information that is so powerful that the world would be awestruck by the depth of our insight and power. Presently, we don't speak with authority to the world because we don't have exclusive information. Our information is the same as theirs with a little religious slant to it; therefore, we are ignored when we speak. What we need is a glorious prophetic insight that arrests the world and causes it to take notice. Access to the Most Holy Place is the missing ingredient in our worship experiences.

This may or may not sound controversial and could possibly be interpreted as going backward to the Old Testament. It may also invoke an immense theological debate. However, just as Martin Luther's theses nailed to the door of the church at Wittenburg invoked a vehement response in the seventeenth century, the debate is expected. However, the debate must begin with the unflattering position of Christianity in this millennium as it is compared to the vibrant body of believers that Jesus left to begin the process in the Acts of the Apostles. Again, we must be forced to examine without prejudice the state of much of the Christian Church, the Body of Christ, and the supernatural manifestation of the presence of YHWH in the modern disciple. The divisions, the contemporary theological perspectives, the powerlessness, the empty worship experiences, and the disillusioned believers should serve as the basis for our concern, not upholding our image and reputation to one another. If we, the Body of Christ, could only humble ourselves and admit our insufficiencies and failures, it would be a great step toward our renovation.

A new and relevant, yet classic (in terms of the unchanging nature of Christ) dimension of worship must be sought by hungry disciples who are tired of basic Sunday entertainment experiences. In my travels from America to the Far East, Europe to Africa and South America, I have found the same attempts by the Church to create something in worship that excites, inspires, and invigorates the worshipers. Whether it comes in the form of catchy musical tunes, contemporary dress codes, fancy building styles, multi-media technology, or creative preaching and teaching, nothing is working to restore the Church permanently to its former luster. Everything has come up short, only producing temporary enthusiasm. Advertising and marketing strategies are constantly being devised to draw new attendees. Pastors are hard-pressed to come up with new things for the church to do in the name of the Lord to attract the downtrodden or the less fortunate. I've recently heard of giveaways in morning services and a couple of pastors who have resorted to giving out money as an incentive to attend worship. Yet we miss the point that YHWH has His own drawing power. His Presence is so irresistible that all you have to do is expose Him to a few people, and they will run and tell the nations where He is and how to find Him. The absurdity of these tactics in light of what worship should represent lets me know that it is time for a revolutionary revelation about worship.

If we can examine the validity of multi-dimensional worship as it relates to the tabernacle pattern, we may begin to please the Father in worship. Since the days of Moses, the Scriptures have not been amended to accommodate our modern times and new theologies. YHWH introduced worship to His people so that there would be no wonder about what He expected us to present to Him in this experience. The Mosaic tabernacle serves as a prophetic pattern, a fixed blueprint that needs no adjustments. That's why He told Moses be sure not to make the slightest adjustment to the pattern based on personal preference or the preference of the people. Furthermore, Hebrews 8:2,5 makes it unquestionable that the earthly tabernacle that Moses erected was indeed a copy of the true tabernacle that pre-existed and was not made by human hands. That simply means that YHWH was establishing for Himself an earthly place of dwelling to match His heavenly place of dwelling. If it was exactly the same on Earth as it was in Heaven, He could come down and make His habitation among people. We in the past have been content with a periodic visitation, but G-d has always been interested in a habitation among people. In Exodus 29:43-46, Jehovah exclaims how He will meet with us and sanctify us and dwell among us so that we will know without question that He is our G-d and we are His people. What a breathtaking reality to live with from day to day.

Once we can reckon with the fact that the pattern and purpose of worship pre-dates us, we must conform to this standard without question. In Genesis 4, this is the reason why Cain's offering is rejected and Abel's is accepted. The modern Christian worship has become like the offering of Cain, we simply have decided to ignore the standard and bring G-d what we feel He should accept. We can conclude from the story of Adam and Eve's redemption that the established standard for satisfying G-d's anger after sin was to slay an innocent animal and allow its blood to speak on our behalf.

Whether understood or not, Adam and Eve saw G-d do this to make coats of skin for them, so we must assume that the practice began with G-d and continued by their own hands from that point on. This would provide for Cain and Abel the acceptable practice for their own worship in the course of time. When Cain and Abel became of age (see Gen. 4:3) and were accountable for their own worship, they were well aware of what G-d wanted. Cain brought an offering with no blood, and Abel brought an offering with blood. What audacity Cain had to do this. He had no respect for G-d, and as a result, G-d had no respect for him. As a matter of fact, the original Hebrew wording suggests that G-d never even saw that he offered anything at all. That is kind of the way I feel about what the contemporary Church does in worship today. We come up with our own innovative and modern styles and liturgies and force them on G-d as if He has to accept it. The reality is that Scripture suggests He doesn't even see that we were in the building. It's some pretty nice fruit that we offer, but it has no sweet-smelling savor to it.

Abel simply brought what He knew G-d wanted, and it was accepted. His offering went up as a sweet-smelling savor before the throne. How easy is it to just give G-d what is already prescribed? He didn't leave it up to us for a reason. He knows what He likes! Our worship must become like the worship of Abel, bringing G-d what He wants. When this happens, it is a universal worship that transcends culture, color, status, and region. It allows us to be "one" here on Earth as a body of believers and not a fragmented group of people who claim we have no barriers between us while every reality contradicts that statement.

The pattern and design of worship exist in Heaven already, and we need not try to invent or re-invent worship. Revelation 11:19 says that the temple of God in Heaven was opened and the Ark of the Covenant was seen in His temple. Reading this Scripture really opened my eyes to a simple truth. The Ark, as well as the temple, pre-existed what Moses was given on the mount. Moses had a copy of the original Ark, and the tabernacle was a shadow of the original temple. Moses had one mandate: Do according to what already exists. Don't adjust it, don't modernize it, don't update it, don't renovate it, and most of all, don't ignore it. It's His house for His glory! The pattern has not changed and will not change forever. At this point, the only one doing any changing is us.

I realize that these are very dramatic and revolutionary concepts being presented; however, they represent what must be done if we are to please YHWH in our corporate worship experiences. We must begin to experience the glory of the Lord in our gatherings. The shekinah must not fall periodically; it must remain in our sanctuaries after we leave. It must be there when we come in and remain when we go out. People must know where G-d dwells and be able to find Him and fellowship with Him on a regular and consistent basis. Worshipers must become priests in their own right and enter into the Most Holy Place with confidence in the shed blood of Christ. They must leave that experience with the conviction to be ambassadors for the Master. They must possess the Holy Spirit and walk in His power and do the things Jesus did when He walked the Earth. Our paradigms must be shifted, and the saints must be empowered in preparation for the return of our Lord and Savior Jesus Christ.

CHAPTER 3

MULTI-DIMENSIONAL MUSIC

Coinciding with the three dimensions of worship are three dimensions of music. As we are well aware, music is a catalyst for worship. In all four corners of the world, you will find music associated with the corporate worship experience. It has served us well to invoke a spiritual atmosphere, and it can often serve as a call to worship. In America, music has become such a vital part of worship that it has become an entity in and of itself. Our musicians and singers have massive followings, and it has led to the creation of an industry and a network of people who have exclusive association based upon their talent. The power of this medium is so popular that there has become a subtle competition between those who lead congregations and those who lead music in those same congregations.

I can remember in my early years of church exposure seeing how the pastor and the musicians or choir director would be at odds right there in morning service. I would always wonder in my immature mind how this could co-exist while we were worshiping G-d. In the Baptist church I grew up in, the musicians would always leave their instrument at the beginning of the sermon and miraculously reappear right as the preacher came to a close. This always seemed strange to me.

Nowadays the music industry giants have become so popular and their following so large that they decided to open churches so as to capitalize on their influence, thus eliminating the competition. The way I grew up, I thought you had to be called to the Gospel ministry, but lately I have seen that if you are popular enough, the power and the people will serve as a sufficient call. Besides, many of these singers realized that they were letting all that money get away on Sunday to their competition, so by having their own churches, they could get the concert money on Saturday night and the tithes on Sunday morning.

Now that music in the Church has become a business, the integrity of why people sing songs about the Lord has been lost. Furthermore, we have declined to the point now where some of the music that we call gospel is now being produced by people who are popular in the music business, but not born-again. This to me has become the most shocking revelation of late. I had to stop buying the music when I began to see that the same names for production or writing were the same ones on the back of a hardcore rap or R&B album. This is part of the reason we have gospel rap, gospel rock, gospel salsa music, and so forth. It is because the producers of worldly music are now the producers of gospel music. Knowing this, I knew that I could not trust the music to produce anything spiritual in me. And that is the point of this chapter. There is a sound for worldly music and another sound for holy music, and the two shall never mix.

The first thing we need to understand is how music became a part of the worship experience because it was not always there. In the original Mosaic experience, there was no music. It was eerily quiet. The only noise heard was the noise of altar fires burning with seething flesh upon it. Whenever Moses or Aaron entered the tabernacle, it was to either hear from YHWH or to tend to the burnt sacrifices and fires that should never cease to burn (see Lev. 6:8-13). This was the standard for tabernacle service and worship for probably a thousand year period. However, there was a practice in the Mosaic period that set the framework for music in worship. It was the inclusion of incense in tabernacle worship.

From the introduction of the tabernacle, G-d included the use of incense to create a sweet smell before His Presence. Exodus 30:1-10 describes the creation of an altar for the burning of incense. Verse 6 says that this altar would be set before the veil that separates the Most Holy Place where the Ark of the Covenant is. The continuing verses state that the burning of incense should be perpetual, that it was Aaron's responsibility to keep it burning, and that he was forbidden to offer strange incense on it. These few verses set the platform for music in worship in the future of the tabernacle. Along with this consideration, we must include the instruction to the perfumer, whose skill and responsibility was to *compose* the incense that would be used before the Presence (see Exod. 30:34-38). These verses give very specific instruction as to the composition and the usage and, in particular, state that it was not to be composed for personal preference or usage. It was a holy substance composed exclusively for the Lord. Please keep these things in mind as we develop the usage of music as it relates to and compares to the usage of incense in the tabernacle worship experience. Finally, the verses conclude by stating that any usage of the incense to satisfy a personal need would bring death upon that person. This is very strong language from the Lord regarding His worship.

We need to now begin to bridge a connection between incense in the Mosaic tabernacle setting and music in the New Testament worship experience. In order to do this effectively we must start with the purpose and characteristics of incense and music in the worship of the Lord.

When we examine the purpose of incense in the Mosaic tabernacle, a few things stand out. First the incense is specifically used before the veil in close proximity to the presence of the Lord. This is an indication that there is an aroma that is appropriate for worship and is also pleasing to G-d. In a way that we are not completely able to understand, aromas are important to G-d. What we do understand from a human perspective is that aromas trigger the mind in particular ways and can even influence the mood of human beings. Modern cosmetology has proven this and uses aroma therapy to create or enhance the well-being of those who use it. If this is true with us, then we can suppose that there may be a similar response from YHWH in this same area or that He wants these aromas to impact us so that we are aware of His holy Presence whenever we sense certain smells.

It was also important that the burning of incense never ceased according to Scripture. This is a clear indication that if the aroma represents a type of worship, then that worship should never cease on Earth as it does not cease around the throne in Glory. Finally, and most importantly, the aroma was a result of a very specific composition of spices. According to Exodus 30:34, the most important factor about the composition is that each ingredient must be in equal amounts. No spice is to outweigh another, thus creating harmony and balance among the ingredients. This particular composition could only be done by someone skilled in the art of perfume making. Without the skill, a person ran the risk of composing something that was not pleasing to the Lord.

Along with the purpose of the incense, we need to examine the characteristics of the incense. Incense possesses very similar characteristics to music. It is invisible. After the initial smoke disappears, you can smell the incense, but you cannot see it. It also fills the space that it is burning in, regardless of how small or large the room. It tends to linger with you even after you have left the location that it was burning in. It impacts or influences the mind in the context that we understand today with regard to aroma therapy. Last but not least, it is composed by someone who is trained with the skill of mixing the right spices and smells to create a harmonious, pleasing scent. All of these characteristics are evident in incense as well as music. It is for these reasons that we are able to equate the inclusion of incense in the Mosaic tabernacle to music in the New Testament worship.

Without this revelation regarding the purpose of incense and the comparative purpose of music in worship, one could think that music has been left in our hands to incorporate into the worship experience. However, once you begin to understand its purpose in worship, you can no longer take lightly the type of music that is played in worship or the composer of that music. In fact, the music should serve as the very last thing you experience in the Inner Court that prepares you to enter into the Most Holy Place. That same music must not be composed for our sake, but for the sake of the one who dwells between the cherubim. This is why we cannot take a melody from a secular song and change the words to make it a gospel song. The original melody was not composed to prepare worshipers to enter into the Most Holy Place.

Now, before we go any further, think of the type of music you are most likely to hear in your church service. Listen closely to the sound. Think of what it does to you mentally and emotionally. What does it produce in you? Does it produce feelings of sadness, antipathy, sympathy, pain, weakness, fear, sensuality, celebration; does it make you want to move your hips and jump around? How does it prepare you to present yourself before the Presence of the Almighty, or does it prepare you for anything in particular? The music that is played in a worship service will either pull you away or draw you to the throne. Even sincere music composed from a genuine Christian perspective will still only have the potential to bring you to the Outer Court. In rare cases, it will bring you to the Inner Court, but because of its composition and musical components, it can take you no farther. Almost all music we hear today in churches contains musical components that the authors are not aware of that hinder the worshiper from reaching the Most Holy Place. I will explain this further in a moment.

First, we must understand how we came to exchange music for incense in the worship experience. I've explain how incense and music possess the same characteristics. So now we need to uncover how the changeover came about.

David is credited with making the permanent transition of incorporating music into the worship experience in First Chronicles 13 (also found in Second Samuel 6). At the point when he brought the Ark back to Jerusalem, there was a great musical celebration in corporate worship. Though his original attempt failed because of ignorance and non-compliance to the pre-existing standards for carrying the Ark, David's second attempt was successful. It is during this second celebration that we see David appointing singers and musicians to *"make a joyful sound"* before the Presence (1 Chron. 15:16 NIV). In particular, he spoke to the Levites, and they appointed their brethren to participate in this area of ministry before the Presence of the Lord. This clarifies who should be qualified for musical leadership in the Church. From the days of Moses, this has not changed. The ministry of the tabernacle and the leadership of worship are distributed between the priest and the Levites. David serves as priest and king (an imagery of Christ) along with the Levites. Thus, there is no competition between the two groups, just as with Moses and Aaron. Each has designated responsibilities and works to complement the other.

Today many churches (and it is commonly accepted) hire musicians and sometimes hire singers, many of whom aren't even members of that local ministry. They simply jump from place to place based upon contracts and monetary offers. Levites are committed to cohesive management of the worship experience alongside the priest. Levites have just as strict a consecration and responsibility on their shoulders (see Exod. 29) to perform their service before the

Lord as the priests. They have a very serious mandate and perform very serious functions in the Inner Court.

After David brought the Ark back into the City of David, the Scripture says he made a tent for it, and this is where the permanent transition took place. For the first time in the history of Israel and its corporate worship experience, the Ark was not returned to the Most Holy Place; it was placed in what is known now as the tabernacle of David. This begins the most dramatic, significant, and prophetic period of corporate worship in the Bible. What David did was unprecedented, and G-d allowed it because David was a man after G-d's own heart.

When he placed the Ark in the tent that he had erected for it, he appointed some of the Levites (the sons of Asaph) to worship before the Ark day and night. It became their full-time occupation to worship before the Presence with verbal praise and thanksgiving and with all types of instruments. Notice that this was a full-time responsibility, which means that worship became their life or their lifestyle. They didn't just worship when they were on duty, because they were known throughout Israel by their occupation. So they become worship, and worship became them. They assumed a posture and life of worship that extended beyond the tabernacle. This is something that we don't see in Church today as we should. David established this group to permanently stand and minister before the Lord, even when everyone else had gone home (see 1 Chron. 16:37-43). They would continue in shifts regularly as required.

What is compelling to me about what David did is that he treated the Ark of the Presence on Earth the same way the Father is treated in Heaven around the throne. He had such great respect for the Presence that he understood that there should not be a time when worship would cease as long as we have His Presence in our midst. In doing this, he made clear that worship is not for the people's enjoyment; worship is for YHWH's enjoyment. Most worship today is people-directed. We sing for the people, we receive offerings for people issues, we have services to commemorate people, and we time the services to accommodate people; everything we seem to do in worship is directed toward the satisfaction of the people. David understood and made sure that the Levites understood that worship is not for us; it is for the Father.

Because David was a worshiper before he was a warrior, his natural inclination was to establish music in the Presence of the Lord. This was what he was accustomed to, and when he implemented this orchestral complement to the corporate worship experience, G-d has no objections. Never before had the Ark sat in an open tent, and never before was there music before the Ark; previously it was behind the veil, and there was only silence and incense before it. It is at this point that music takes the place of incense in purpose and character to go before the Lord's presence. If music is to go before the Ark of the Presence, then it also means that the responsibility for setting the atmosphere before the Presence is now shifted from the fragrance of an inanimate object to that of a living being—the Levite.

This should give us foundation for not only the purpose of music in worship, but also the character of music in worship. With this understanding, I can now return to the aforementioned issue of why most music today actually hinders the worshiper from entering into the Most Holy Place in particular and often creates difficulty in entering the Inner Court.

There are three dimensions of original worship as patterned in the Mosaic tabernacle setup. As previously mentioned, these are the Outer Court, Inner Court (Holy Place), and the Most Holy Place. For each dimension, there is a corresponding musical sound that supports that dimension of worship. Most musicians and singers are completely unaware of this reality, and this is most unfortunate. They think that the catchier the tune, the louder or softer the music, the more talented the band or singer, the greater the music serves the worship experience. Most church music is completely culturally sensitive. This means that the sounds we hear on Sunday are very similar in composition and flavor to the sounds we hear in our secular culture. Black churches have R&B, blues, jazzy, or rap sounds to the music. Many Caucasian churches can have a pop, rock/heavy metal, country, Broadway show, or classical music sound. Latin churches vary from pop, salsa, or meringue sounds. And Asian, European, and Indian churches follow similar trends regarding popular music and cultural native sounds.

What we may or may not realize is that each of these cultural sounds will influence to a large degree who feels comfortable in the pews. This is the main reason why so many churches are single culture experiences. The churches that have a cross-over appeal typically ascribe to cross-over music styles. Now what we have to look at are two things. First, is this G-d's original intent in regard to music in corporate worship? (We know the answer to that is *no*.) And second, do these compositions serve to prepare worshipers to enter into the Presence of the Almighty?

As previously stated, the first dimension of worship is the worship of the sinner. In this dimension, the worshiper must deal with his sin based upon the actions of his flesh. It is in this dimension of worship that we are constantly reminded of our flesh and its failure to submit completely to the will of G-d. The sound and composition of music in this dimension is dominated by rhythm. Music that is dominated by rhythm is typically distinguished by a strong beat and is characterized by drums and percussion. Rhythm appeals to the flesh; the more dominating the rhythm, the more the body reacts. Outer Court music is dominated by rhythm and keeps people conscious of their flesh. This is why in night clubs, secular concerts, and parties the bass and drum lines are so strong. The music is supposed to create an atmosphere of carnality and sensuality. While worshiping with strong rhythmic tunes, a person is reminded of the flesh. This is why a person can go to a church service and leave feeling sensual and unsatisfied spiritually and proceed to be satisfied carnally immediately after the service. This can be manifest in sexuality, in overeating, in shopping, or in the need to do anything that gives the flesh comfort.

The composition of such music can never prepare you to enter into the Holy Place. This is why there is no such thing as gospel rap or Christian rock. It is impossible to prepare someone for a higher dimension of worship while appealing to the flesh. Flesh begets flesh, as Jesus stated to Nicodemus (see John 3:6). Once we reckon with the fact that the very composition of some music hinders the dimension of worship we are able to enter into, then we will automatically eliminate some music from our worship experiences. Keep in mind that this is the same area that Lucifer had jurisdiction over in Heaven. He is well aware of its importance as it relates to the celebration of the Father; he will not relinquish his stronghold over this area easily. This is his entry point into the worship experience. It is frightening to think that we can gather for worship in our churches and actually give the enemy a full space in that service to influence and distract people from the worship of the Father and no one knows it. He authors and births forms of music, compositions, and chords, and then he introduces them to the world and makes them popular. Then he influences some naïve Christian singers and musicians and gets them to buy into the secular styles for the sake of popularity. Next thing we know, the sound of the world is right in the Church, wooing people away from the Holy Place into a carnal place, all the while thinking that this worship is pleasing to G-d. What we need in our worship experiences today is a sound that comes from above and not below.

In order to accomplish this sound, we must first apply the pattern of composition as it is compared to the composition of the incense in the Old Testament tabernacle experience. The sounds we hear today are typically imbalanced rhythmically. One part of the music typically outweighs another part of the music, which causes it to have a particular effect on the hearer. When the incense was composed, the Lord commanded that no ingredient outweigh another; each one was to be in equal quantity to the other. This would mean that the composition of music is the same. No part of the music should be more pronounced or overbearing than another part. In other words, if the percussion outweighs the brass or the brass outweighs the strings, the music will have the potential to influence the hearer in one way or another. One might call this extreme, but we must remember, just as YHWH stated, that the incense was not for personal use or satisfaction; neither is the music we compose. The music is not to cater to us; it is to cater to Him.

After teaching a lesson on music at a seminar once, one of the attendees came up to me and stated emphatically that I was in error. She asked, "What would this music sound like if it did not have components that we are familiar with?" My response to her was that we must seek the Lord for the sound that is pleasing to Him and not bring Him what was founded by Lucifer and his followers. I told her that, just as secular music is birthed through a process of "seeking," so too we are responsible to "seek the Lord" and get our sound from Him. She was baffled.

Rap/hip hop music was birthed by people who took the time to meditate until they came up with something original; why should the Church take the easy way out and simply piggyback off of the secular world's effort? Are we so lazy that we can't take the time to meditate and ask the Lord for a sound that is original and uniquely represents the sound Heaven is pleased with? We have a mandate to discover that sound and compose it like incense before the Presence of the Lord so that it will create an atmosphere that is pleasing and inviting to Him.

Since music dominated by the rhythm or beat will keep us in the flesh and in the Outer Court, we must balance out the sound of all the music we use for worship as a first step. We must not lean upon a base line or a strong percussion section to get the worshipers excited and moving; that is the job of the Holy Spirit. If we are able to create balance in the sound of the music, we create an opportunity for the worshiper to enter into the next dimension of worship. The music doesn't drive them there; the Holy Spirit invites them there. The goal of worship is to get to the Most Holy Place. In order to make the transitions from the Outer Court smooth, the music has to be designed with this goal in mind. The music will help or hinder this process.

The second dimension of worship is "the worship of the saints," which is accomplished in the Inner Court or the Holy Place. The sound that goes with this dimension is dominated by harmony. Harmony is blended sounds characterized by diverse notes. Harmony reminds the worshiper of the soul. When composers are able to take diverse notes on a scale and bring them together successfully to accomplish an acceptable sound, it is pleasing to the soul. The success of blending these sounds actually makes the composer proud. So the soul can boast in the achievement of this unique sound. Music that is dominated by harmony will keep the worshiper in the Inner Court.

Now it is important to note that the Church spends a lot of time in the Holy Place for the purpose of instruction, intercession, and preparation. So the worship that takes place in this dimension is very important. We do not rush through this season of our worship, so it is not entirely negative that music be composed to maintain worship at this level. Ministry to the soul is valuable if we are going to have self-assessment and examination before we go into the Most Holy Place. However, we have to be careful to recognize that the music must help the saint to deal with the soul and not become proud and puffed up at the soul's accomplishments. Often times, when we are experiencing beautiful, harmonious music, we can tend to not see our flaws and failures or our need to continue to move forward, because we feel so good about where we are at that moment.

The other thing we must be aware of is that the soul, or *psuche* in Greek, deals with the psyche or the mind. When the music ministers to the mind, it can create psychological connections that can be confusing or sentimental. What I mean is that the connections that are accomplished while making harmony create a bond that can be confusing later. Whenever two or more human beings work well together to bring about harmony of any sort, they have to be careful that they don't confuse that achievement with an unnecessary emotional or sentimental attachment. If they confuse their achievement as something more, they run the risk of becoming romantic or passionate toward each other inappropriately. On the Mount of Transfiguration, harmony was accomplished among the four participants so much so that Peter wanted to stay there forever. However, G-d spoke to shake him out of this inappropriate passion by saying to Peter, "This is not about you; hear My Son" (see Matt. 17:1-5).

Oftentimes, after achieving harmony, we tend to shift our focus from G-d to ourselves. This is why music is so risky for humans in worship. Once we create a great sound or compose a beautiful song, those who hear it begin to esteem us, and most times we accept and enjoy it. This is the catalyst that shifts our focus off of pleasing the Father with our music and causes us to desire to be acknowledged for our harmony and perfection. Since this type of music appeals to the soul, we must make sure that the music works on the soul to bring it to a place where it is useful in worship. According to First Thessalonians 5:23, the soul can be sanctified; therefore, even if we are making music for the Inner Court, it should inspire the sanctification of the soul in preparation for entry into the Most Holy Place.

This harmonious and balanced sound will be instrumental in ministering to people's souls, and this is valuable. When the soul is touched by song, we must be aware that people open themselves up spiritually at that time. They become aware of something that the song dealt within them. They become appreciative to the composer of the music, and the composer holds a special place in their hearts at that time. The composers and singers must be aware of this fact so as not to create any further confusion in the people being ministered to. They must immediately redirect the people to G-d if they become overly sentimental toward them.

We see this confusion often in the contemporary Church. As a result of this connection, singers and musicians develop a following because of their music. The followers play their music all the time in their cars and in their homes and sometimes in their churches. Next there becomes an inordinate affection. As a result of this sentimental and confusing attachment, these people are open to exploitation. Next the musicians or singers become celebrities whom you have to pay to see, and they only minister their music based upon financial contracts and incentives. This would not be the case if, while ministering to the soul of the worshiper, they redirected the affection and sentiment to the Lord. This also has a lot to do with the competition most churches experience between the pastor and the minister of music. Both parties are dealing with the soul of the worshiper, and both are creating or encouraging an affectionate relationship. As a result, both become confused about those who worship in that church and begin to compete for their allegiance. This, in turn, causes conflict right there in the midst of any given worship service.

Worship leaders, pastors, musicians, and singers must be aware that the goal of the worship experience is not to capture the attention of the worshiper personally, but rather to lead or direct that worshiper to the next dimension of worship. When this is the motive of the leadership, there will be no inordinate affections, no inappropriate sentiment, and no confusion exhibited by the worshiper in regard to why this wonderful atmosphere is being supplied. They and the leadership will know that the music composition is provided as an entry point to another dimension, as incense before the veil provides the ambiance that makes YHWH comfortable and serves as the entry point to the Most Holy Place.

Harmony is necessary to achieve great sounding music. Music that does not flow in some type of harmony sounds chaotic. In America, we experienced something like this at the end of the soul and bebop jazz eras; we strayed into a strange music type called fusion, which also contributed to the hard rock sound. Basically, it was music that had no sensible harmony. Obviously, when we compare the composition of music to the composition of the incense, we understand that there was harmony between the spices that were used. Only certain spices mixed harmoniously with other spices to create the perfect scent. So it is important that we acknowledge this powerful mixture in music to create the appropriate sound before the Lord. However, we must keep in mind that whenever we achieve this type of perfect harmony, we run the risk of taking credit for it. We also can't help but feel like our efforts, talents, and voices have accomplished this on our own. When this happens, it opens the door for pride and self-exaltation, which would prohibit us from entering into the Most Holy Place. As long as we keep in mind that this harmony is accomplished in hopes of pleasing the Father and preparing the saints for the next dimension, we will be okay.

The main thing is to deflect the attention and glory away from ourselves at these times. This is a difficult thing to do when the people tend to see the leaders and respond to their talents or gifts. However, it can be accomplished with proper teaching and practice. As we instill these thoughts into the minds of the worshipers on a continuous basis, they will begin to enforce it on their own. When we minister to the souls of the worshipers harmoniously, we are doing the work of the incense in the Old Testament tabernacle setting. Just as the smell jars the memory and takes the mind on a journey to the place or time it was first experienced, so must the harmonious sound be to the hearer. This is why it ministers to the soul. It is designed and composed to take the mind to a particular place, and that place should minister healing and deliverance to the hearer. The worshiper cannot enter the Most Holy Place in the flesh, so it is important that the music crucify the flesh and minister to the soul in preparation for entry to the next level.

Last but not least, when this is accomplished, the worship leader must be discerning enough to know when to get out of the way. There is a time in worship when the ministry to the soul must cease. Unfortunately, when we start ministering to the soul, we never want to stop because we are getting such a strong and emotional response. This is deceptive. Since the Church is now so oriented toward thinking that the goal of ministry is to get an emotional response from the people, we get to that point, and we work it to physical exhaustion. This is not the goal. In this dimension, we must keep in mind that when we come to the end of our ability to minister to the soul, we must move out of the way so that the worshiper can then go into the area of the ministry in the spirit to the Lord. This is paramount in corporate worship.

In order to diminish the confusion and sentiment that is directed toward a human being, discerning leaders will disappear when they sense it coming on. They must be effective in ministering powerfully to the soul and getting the worshipers to open themselves up to the Almighty. When the leaders see that this process is fully exhausted, their job is to transition the worship from the Inner Court to the Most Holy Place. At this point, the worshipers move from the dimension for the worship of the saints to the dimension of the worship of the Lord.

I've seen this happen over and over again in my ministry, and it is truly rewarding and releasing when it happens. There is nothing more satisfying than to know that you have done your job properly. When the saints have been ministered to by the appropriate harmonious sounds, they are released within themselves to be open to the Lord without restriction, and then they are directed to the Most Holy Place so that they may worship YHWH face-to-face without the influence of people. These are the goals and precautions of harmonious music.

Finally, when we go to the highest levels in worship, there is one more sound that must be discovered. This is the sound that takes us into the Most Holy Place—the dimension of the worship of the Lord.

Music in the third dimension is dominated by melody. It is not a harmonious sound of blended notes or singers; it is a solitary sound. This music is characterized by single notes that create the foundation for a song. There is no percussion of rhythmic accompaniment. One would call it simple and unsophisticated. It is accomplished by one person making a melody in the heart. A melody fingered on a piano or organ doesn't have a polished sound, but still puts the hearer in the mind of the words of the song. In fact, when it is fingered simplistically, it is less distracting and causes the mind to fill in the necessary components. Melody appeals to the spirit and fosters entry into the presence of the Almighty. Melody doesn't necessarily need harmony and certainly doesn't need rhythm. Melody is where every song begins; it is embellished by harmony and rhythm for our satisfaction, but the melody is sufficient by itself to minister to the spirit. Worship often reaches its highest levels when it is melodious. Why is this important, and how does it relate to worship in the Most Holy Place?

One of the characteristics of worship in the Most Holy Place is that when the priest went in, there was no one else present, which means there was no human influence. It was a very intimate and personal experience. There were no distractions, and all of the attention was on the Ark of the Covenant, the place of the Presence. The other dimensions of worship do not accomplish this; however, they should prepare us for this. After dealing with the distraction of the flesh in the Outer Court and putting it aside and then dealing with the soul and instructing it in the Inner Court, the spirit now has a chance to enjoy the presence of the Lord uninterrupted in the Most Holy Place. The sound in the Most Holy Place is singular just like a melody played or hummed in simplicity. It has no accompaniment and no percussion, thus diminishing the activity of the flesh and the soul. It represents a singular sound coming from a singular person.

As your spirit connects with G-d, it no longer needs embellishments as in the other dimensions.

Have you ever been in a worship service where suddenly the drums ceased, the singers quieted their voices, and there was a serene type of sound going forth with only voices of worshipers in the background? This was a moment when the people had ascended to the Most Holy Place; they were in the presence of YHWH, and they needed no human influence.

Typically our insecurities don't allow these moments to last too long. Depending on the level of maturity and security of the leadership, often someone will get nervous and jump to the microphone to move the service along or interrupt the moment with a fleshly influence. What most leadership doesn't realize is that these moments should not be a strange phenomenon, but rather what we expect from Sabbath to Sabbath.

I also need to note that melodies are often timeless from a musical perspective. The timing or lack thereof is left to the one creating the melody. This is important because timing typically invokes the participation of drums or percussion instruments. When timing is absent, there is no need for percussion. I believe timeless music is divine and brings a heavenly context with it because there is no timing in Heaven. Since Heaven is a timeless environment, there is no need for percussion instruments in Heaven. Drums are really only needed to keep some type of timing to the music. However, as previously stated, the consequence of using drums, percussion, and rhythm is that it will empower the flesh. Music in the Most Holy Place could not be rhythmic because that would be counterproductive to the environment. This is why I say that some music, just based upon its composition, hinders us from moving to a higher dimension of worship. Though it may sound good and get a demonstrative response from the listeners, it will not bring them to the highest form of worship.

There is a sound, a melodious sound, simple and singular in composition, that allows us not to focus on the composer or how it ministers to us, but allows us to focus on the one for whom the sound was created. It is this sound that we need to compose to not only please the Almighty, but to also enhance the atmosphere that the worshiper must enter into to experience the highest form of worship in the Earth realm. This sound causes the worshiper to see nothing and no one other than the Lord Most High. When this is achieved, the spirits of people will connect, bond, and become sentimental toward the Spirit of G-d.

This sound is not taken from worldly songs; it is not driven by what is contemporary, and it is not birthed out of a desire to make money or become popular through the music. This sound comes from consecrated lives that have become quiet before the Lord and have allowed Him to dictate to them what He wants to hear. The sound is not for us, though we will enjoy it; the sound is for YHWH. There are no shortcuts to creating music in this context. Music in this context is composed out of one singular revelation. That understanding is the original intent of the Father when He gave corporate worship to the children of Israel, and it shows us how to continue in that discipline in the modern age without compromise.

It is so unfortunate that the corporate worship experience has been so twisted that in the modern age we believe that we are supposed to be blessed by the worship. Yet in the days of Moses, everyone sought to please Adonai with their worship. According to Deuteronomy, they would sit in their tent doors and wait to see if the Lord was pleased by their presentation based upon what Moses said of the Lord. If the purpose and direction of ministry is changed, then the music that is produced for that atmosphere will be changed also. The music we hear today is largely composed to accommodate the purpose and direction of modern ministry. The direction is now pointed toward us and not G-d.

These perspectives will save us from struggling through unsuccessful and unsatisfying music ministries. However you choose to view it, you must reckon with the winds of change that are coming. These winds are not a breeze; they are a hurricane. The only things standing after a hurricane must have had an unshakeable foundation. Today's music is on shaky ground to say the least. It has the wrong motivations and accomplishes superficial results. It is time that we demand more from worship music than just clapping hands and gyrating bodies; worship music should take us to a place we have never been before in worship. When it achieves those kinds of results, it will be just the beginning of what G-d desires from us and for us in worship.

CHAPTER 4

THE THRESHING FLOOR OF ORNAN

David is undeniably the key figure in the Old Testament when it comes to worship. He is singularly responsible for implementing the transition that is still largely in place to this day. It is necessary to understand some of the evolution of David's adult life in order to acquaint ourselves with a true and authentic worship experience.

Though David was groomed to be a worshiper in his adolescence, he became known as a warrior in his adulthood. I believe his preoccupation with war kept him from focusing all of his attention on creative worship. This is why bringing the Ark of the Covenant back to Jerusalem became such a monumental event for him personally. It was a sign and demonstration that he was transitioning back to worship as a focus of his life and the life of the nation. The Bible says that he danced with all his might before the Lord during that celebration. What a release David must have been experiencing as he not only reminisced about his youthful days of worship, but also felt that he was moving back to a place where he would not be as focused on war as much as worship. This in and of itself is key in the development of a new worship paradigm.

The Bible states in Second Samuel 7:1 that when the Lord had given him rest from his enemies, his attention shifted. It was at this point that David, while sitting in his house of cedar, became concerned about the place where the Ark abode. What happened to David must happen in the life of the Church so that it can move to a new dimension of worship. David rested from his enemies. The Church has not rested from its enemies. This is a tactic used by Satan to keep the Church distracted from its ultimate and paramount purpose in the Earth. Our battles tend to be ongoing and continuous; we tend to go from one battle to the next without a chance to regroup. Some pastors and ministry leaders burn out simply because they never get to rest. Not only are our enemies distracting, but they cause the type of worship we produce to be in direct relationship to our battles. What this does is take the attention off of YHWH and put it on our latest struggle, thereby glorifying the struggle. We don't even recognize it anymore because we are so used to it. We sing about how far down we fell or how destitute we were or how broken we felt at certain times of our lives. Ultimately these songs end with a chorus or a phrase that is encouraging. However, the object of the song is the enemy of our souls. That enemy can be sickness, stress, scandal, financial difficulty, relationship issues, and the like; and these things are the motivation for writing the song. What we fail to realize is that resting from our enemy will produce a different song with a different object and focus.

David rested from his enemies, and the first thing that came to his mind was worship. It was not worship to encourage his distressed soul or lift his heart from despair, but something he could do for the G-d of Heaven simply because his mind was free to think that way now. His first thought was creative and unprecedented. He said that the Ark should have a more glorious dwelling place than he did, a permanent place that Israel could worship in forever. This had never happened before. Where did David get this thought from? Why was he thinking this way in regard to worship? What was in his heart that made him come up with such an audacious scheme? A further reading of the chapter gives a little insight into some alternative reasons that may have played into it; however, what we can definitively conclude is that David rested from his distractions and got back to what was paramount in his life. This was the inspiration for a new and creative way of thinking about worship.

As a result of David desiring to do this for the Presence, Nathan the prophet said to David without hesitation, *"Do all that is in your heart; for God is with you"* (1 Chron. 17:2). Though Nathan had to recant this statement later, I love this proclamation. What it establishes for me is that, because David was a true worshiper and a man after G-d's own heart, there were no restrictions laid upon him when it came to his passion: worship. What I believe the Scripture is indicating for us today is that there is no restriction on those who have a pure and undefiled desire to please him in worship. YHWH reads and knows our hearts, and in this context, He puts *His* desire in *our* hearts so that we can carry it out with freedom and passion.

The timing of David's desire coincided with some divine and natural realities. One is that G-d had already appointed a place for permanent earthly worship to be established. Two is that Israel was established in a permanent territory and would not be moving nomadically any longer; therefore, the portable tabernacle of Moses had become obsolete. Three, as previously stated, is that they had come to an end of enemy oppression due to David's valiant ability to destroy his enemies. These strategic realities were keys in the transition of worship in that era.

Similarly I believe we are strategically living in a time when worship must return to its foundations, the Church must be positioned properly and powerfully for the return of Christ, and the world must have a real and authentic alternative to powerless and fruitless religions. A new worship paradigm will be key in establishing an environment for the Lord's return in this the third day since the revelation of Christ to the Earth. It is this collision of time and purpose that created destiny for David and will create destiny for this new dimension of worship.

What becomes obvious while studying this era of David's life is that G-d has already decided upon an eternal, earthly location for a permanent worship facility. We can see this in hindsight through the Scriptures. However, when David goes through a series of events in his personal life, he is not aware as to how these events bring him to the place of the Lord's worship. The reason why this is important for us is because so often Christians deem themselves unworthy because of some mistakes or embarrassments in their past. Yet when you look at the life of David, it is filled with mistakes and embarrassing situations, and G-d still used him (and his experiences) to be a catalyst for a new dimension of worship in the Earth. Fortunately for us, just as with David, we can point to no personal achievements of our own as a qualification for G-d to use us. For if this was the case, we would diminish or ignore the grace and sovereignty of G-d. We would also think that we had become worthy on our own merits and thus lord our merits over others. G-d knows that we possess this weakness of the flesh so He allows us to have calamities, mistakes, and embarrassments so that we are sure to acknowledge the great grace in our lives as the reason why He continues to use us. David's life, like ours, was filled with reasons why G-d could have disqualified him; yet as we will see, even the negative things worked to ultimately fulfill G-d's plan in the Earth.

What is fascinating is that David's error progresses into G-d's intentions. In First Chronicles 21, the Bible states that David (by the provocation of Satan) decides to number G-d's people. Even with the challenge of Joab, David's word prevails and the people are numbered. Though we can only speculate as to why David insisted on numbering the people, we know that pride and ego had a lot to do with it. As a result, it was credited to David as a sin to do what he did.

While reading the text, you almost feel like David had a brief mental lapse when he did this. YHWH's response was swift against Israel, and David quickly realized that he had made a grave error. The brevity of this part of the story can almost make one believe that, though David was obviously in the wrong, something else was going on behind the scenes. Why was Satan so blatantly involved with this incident? Why wasn't David more discerning or sensitive to the words of Joab? Why didn't G-d smite David for his error? Why did He smite Israel? These few questions lead me to believe that G-d was going to use a negative situation to bring into place His ultimate plan in the Earth. Let me be careful to mention that only an omniscient G-d could manage to cause an evil situation to serve as a catalyst for a superior plan.

As a result of David's failure, he was quick to recognize it and repent. He took ownership and was willing to pay the price for his sin. Whether this is designed to simply humble David or whether there was more to it, I am not sure. What I do understand is that G-d was about to do something amazing and eternal in the life of David, and maybe it was necessary for David to go through a severely humiliating experience as a precursor for the exaltation that was coming his way. It was because of this failure that David was put into a predicament with the Father. Gad, his seer, presented David with three options as to how penance would be made with Heaven. He was told that he could have the Earth revolt against him for three years via famine, people could successfully defeat him for three months, or Heaven could come against him for three days. David chose wisely to fall into the hands of the G-d he worshiped.

This is an aspect of the worshiper's life that cannot be discounted. David worshiped the One he knew and trusted in all circumstances and predicaments. There is a foundational trust that is built when one is a worshiper that never goes away. So often in our modern theology and in our contemporary worship, we don't find a continuous confidence being built up. People can be in church all their lives and say that they are saved just as long, sing in the choir, serve in a ministry, hold a position with a title, and yet with every passing predicament, they fall out of confidence with the G-d they claim to worship.

David's choice suggests that he not only worshiped the G-d of Heaven, but knew the G-d he worshiped. He was confident that he was not just a subject of YHWH's anger, but rather an intimate participant in YHWH's plan. So it didn't matter more that he had made a mistake than it did that he was intimately involved in the history of Israel and Adonai. We tend to make our mistakes so paramount that they actually become idolatrous and hinder our understanding of how the Father's plans will always supersede our shortcomings. If this were not the case, then who on Earth could G-d use to fulfill His purposes in the Earth? Worshipers are more G-d-conscious than they are mistake-conscious. This allows them to keep their eyes on Heaven even when Earth is out of order.

As a result of David's choice, YHWH authorizes an angel to move destructively through Jerusalem. This is where the story becomes fascinating and revealing at the same time. G-d is viewing the destruction as it takes place and is affected by the site of the devastation, so He commands the angel to restrain his hand. At the point of this instruction, the angel ceases his activity at a particular location: the threshing floor of Ornan the Jebusite. This is not accidental.

Let me reiterate what I began with in the beginning of this chapter. When David rested from his enemies, he got back to where his heart and passion were: worship. David stated that he had a desire to build a house for the Ark of the Presence. This is where we began our thoughts. At the point of David's sincere desire, David's transitioning of how corporate worship looked, and the changing of an era in Israel's life in that they are no longer nomadic—G-d was behind this collision of personal destiny, national providence, and divine ordinance. The problem with David's desire to build a house for the

Lord was that he would have no idea where to build it on his own. He would be completely unaware by natural means to know if there was a location previously designated by Heaven as the place for such a glorious temple. This in and of itself would mean that G-d would have to reveal to David where this temple was to be built or at least set in motion a series of events that would cause David to have an eternal allegiance to such a location. This is exactly what happened in the chronicle.

According to First Chronicles 21:16-17, at this very point, David lifted his eyes, saw the angel with sword drawn, and began to plead for mercy for the sake of the people. His sincere plea got him an immediate response from David's seer Gad by the instruction of the angel. Gad told David that he should go and erect an altar to the Lord at the place where the angel stood—the threshing floor of Ornan.

At the same time that this was happening, Ornan was actually threshing wheat at this particular location. Strangely enough, he saw the angel and did not fear, but continued threshing the wheat. This is indeed a cause for curiosity; however, verses 21 and 23 give us some insight into the character of Ornan. Firstly, he is one who honored authority. His posture toward David signifies that he gave honor to those who deserved honor by bowing down before David, regardless of what the nation was going through. This is noteworthy. Secondly, he further emphasized that honor by being willing to give the property and the provisions for sacrifice to the king in response to his simple request for it. This again speaks to the spirit of the man and shows his fear of the Lord and his respect for the Lord's servant. I imagine this is why he did not panic when he saw the angel of the Lord with his sword drawn. Ornan's posture was that of an upright man who feared the Lord, and he knew that neither the angel nor the sword were against him.

King David approached Ornan and insisted upon purchasing the location at full price for the purpose of erecting an altar for worship and thus removing the plague that had come upon Israel. Now David was driven by a need to pay a price for what he had done, so though Ornan was willing to give it to him, along with sacrifices, for free, David knew that he would feel unfulfilled in his repentance if this didn't cost him something. This is a wonderful demonstration of a leader who is willing to own up to his error and suffer the expense for those same mistakes. This is not typical in our culture today, but David was a true worshiper and would not be satisfied any other way. The G-d he worshiped was the same G-d he was willing to face when he was in the wrong. This confidence can only be built and established by a true worshiper.

While David insisted that he could not offer to G-d that which cost him nothing, something else was at work here. If David were to accept this location as a gift and not own it by virtue of a purchase, there would remain a possibility that after David's death (or Ornan's) there could be a dispute over who had the rights to the property and what it should be used for. David was compelled by his desire to offer to G-d something that included his personal sacrifice, but at the same time, G-d foresaw that this location would be the key to eternal worship in the Earth and that the property must be deeded to David the worshiper. As a result of David's immediate worship and sacrificing, G-d answered by fire from Heaven to confirm His acceptance of David's worship. Once this happened, the angel returned his sword to his sheath and the plague was over.

At this point, David was moved in the same way that other patriarchs were moved. When they saw G-d or an angel or received revelation from the Lord in a particular way, they memorialized that place. David was no different. He recognized the place as special or significant, and he sacrificed there, again! And notice what the Scripture says about why he did what he did, *"For the tabernacle of the Lord...*[was] *at the high place in Gibeon"* (1 Chron. 21:29). Because of inconvenience and fear of the angel, G-d initiated the shift away from the Mosaic tabernacle to this location, not by accident, but by divine providence. This shift is most fascinating and paramount as to where worship is today. I will address it in detail in the next chapter. Nevertheless, the location now becomes the focal point of David's worship because it is the place that he will always remember as a place of mercy toward him and all of Israel.

The angel in this case can be viewed as a clear sign from YHWH that He did not want David to return to the old place of worship, thus substantiating that it was indeed time for something new. I'm not sure if the modern Church has been able to adapt to this kind of divine intervention yet. It might have a lot to do with our pride and ego, but it is a fault of our present experience. We tend to insist on things continuing in the way that we are familiar with, whether there is a road block or not. For David, the angel with the sword was enough to convince him that sacrificing in this new location is not sacrilegious. As a matter of fact, the Scripture, beginning in the next chapter, makes it clear that David had completely embraced that new location by calling it *"the house of the Lord God"* (1 Chron. 22:1). From that point on, he commenced to put everything in place to prepare the great house that would be built on that exact spot.

The location that is the threshing floor of Ornan should not be looked upon lightly. A threshing floor was typically used to thresh out wheat. As a matter of fact, at the point that Ornan saw the angel and all that was going on, that is exactly what he was doing. The word for "threshing" in the Hebrew means "to trample, break, or tear down." It is also typically located on a high, flat plateau so that the wind can blow away the chaff of the wheat. It is significant that this was the place where G-d chose for the angel to direct David's attention to. Certainly David was going through a breaking experience in his life at this very moment. So he came to the threshing floor so that he could be broken and the chaff (the superficial) could be removed from his life. How important is this in the life of the worshiper? It is invaluable to digest this lesson. David didn't lose his status as a worshiper because of his sin. However, David went through a process of breaking so that he could go to the next level of worship and obedience with the Father.

We tend to miss this lesson in the modern Christian experience, or at least we attempt to avoid it. With David it was unavoidable because it was all a part of the ultimate plan—the ego, the temptation to number the people, the consequence, the proper attitude in repentance, and the arrival at the place that he may not ever have arrived at if it were not for this uncanny series of events. In moving to a new place of worship, the Church must be able to go through a threshing floor experience. We must be willing to be broken and trampled on. We must be willing to be embarrassed and ashamed for our actions. We must be willing to pay a price for our mistakes, and we must reckon with the ultimate plan that is indeed a result of all of this confusion and error.

One of the joys of the threshing floor experience is that when you come through it, you only possess what really matters. All of the superficial, cosmetic exterior is removed. You can always tell when someone has gone through a real breaking. They are no longer concerned with those little things that used to mean so much to them in the past. They spend less time and money on the things that simply support their ego or reputation. They impute fewer demands on those around them to accommodate their idiosyncrasies. In essence, they exhibit brokenness and humility. After this experience, David went back to what he was most concerned with when he rested from his enemies: worship. He immediately moved to establish in that location a house of worship for the Lord. And this location that David had been drawn to had deep implications in the history of Israel. So for G-d to bring David to this location through these strange and unusual circumstances clearly conveys the greatness of our G-d and the greatness of His plan.

This threshing floor or Ornan has traditionally been identified as Mount Moriah, and this mount has great significance in the life of Israel. Genesis 22 describes the story of the testing of Abraham regarding the life of his son Isaac. According to the text, he was directed to Mount Moriah to worship. This worship would include the sacrificing of his only son, and as we know, Abraham proceeded to that mountaintop in faith. The Bible specifically says that YHWH showed him the place that he was to make this sacrifice. Abraham was led to this place and did not know it before YHWH made it known to him. This is a key in understanding worship. We do not know the place or practice that pleases G-d until He shows us. Without His express input, we have no idea what to offer Him.

Abraham gets to the place of YHWH's choosing (Mount Moriah), and he offers to G-d what He asks for and not what he has decided to give Him. In the process of Abraham preparing to offer Isaac, G-d intervenes and provides for Himself another sacrifice. YHWH then comments with admiration that now He knows that Abraham is willing to give Him whatever He asks for in worship, down to his only son. This is clearly what G-d is looking for from us today, the willingness to give Him whatever He asks for in worship. Whether we understand it or not, we must just give Him whatever He asks for.

The provision in this story is obviously a sign of the provision that would come to fruition in the days of David. David had no idea how this plague would come to an end, so G-d Himself provided the solution by supplying the angel and the threshing floor as the conduit for David moving back to his original plan of building a house for the Lord. I believe that G-d will do whatever He has to do to bring the blood-bought Church back to the place of worship He originally intended for us. He will provide the information, motivation, and application of His purposes so that He can receive the worship He desires from the inhabitants of the earth.

Knowing that G-d brought David through all of this just so that He could reestablish this place of worship in the Earth is awesome. It gives me confidence to know that this is where we are today. Christianity is a mess, universally speaking. We are so far from what Christ intended when He departed that there is really only one solution now. He must, by His own means, provide for us a way to get back to Him. Based upon David's experience, it will not be pretty, but it will be effective. I'm sure that we will end up at the threshing floor, willing to be broken down so that we can have a chance at becoming valuable and meaningful again.

By all accounts, this experience was so life-changing for David that for the rest of his life he was completely focused on the preparations for this glorious temple, even though he knew that he would not build the physical structure. The preparations were extensive, and his son Solomon was inexperienced and would be overwhelmed by the task if David didn't provide the framework. So the balance of First Chronicles describes the details for the physical structure as well as the ministry that would take place within that structure.

Most of our churches today that enter into a building program spend a great deal of time with the physical planning. The architect, builder, contractors, blueprints, cost, and the like tend to consume the leader. Then, after the project is completed, they bring an old and antiquated ministry format into the new structure as if the building will make the worship more authentic. This was not the case with David. David started the process by giving instruction and preparation to the Levites, the priest, the gatekeepers, the musicians, and the order of the ministry so that the order of the house would exceed the glory of the physical structure. We see proof of this in Second Chronicles when the Queen of Sheba fainted as Solomon ascended the temple to go into worship. This response from the Queen of Sheba was clearly a response to the order, excellence, and precision of the ascent to worship. Solomon's preparation and presentation of worship was awe-inspiring, not because of the magnitude of the structure, but because of the way in which Solomon and his servants approached the place of the Presence.

David, like so many of our modern-day pastors, originally intended on building a structure that would memorialize his legacy for generations to come. However, when G-d redirected him, he understood that it was not his personal legacy that needed to be established in the Earth in the natural. Rather, it was a spiritual legacy that G-d would establish eternally that would mark the life of David for generations to come. That spiritual legacy would be one of Davidic worship released into the Earth through his life and devotion that G-d would use in our day to bring the Church back to His original intentions of corporate and private worship.

Many a magnificent structure has been built only to signify the greatness of the leader of that congregation. As a result, the legacy is limited to bricks and mortar. Pastoral leadership must catch the vision that what G-d is doing in the Body of Christ will exceed them and their time spans. We tend to function from such a limited view of how the Father works through His vessels that we diminish the great work of the kingdom to a few people whom we deem worthy of participation. David's preparation after this incident clarifies his new perspective of the kingdom process. He would release all of his resources: wisdom, finances, authority, and experience so that his once considered illegitimate son would carry on the great work of the kingdom without interruption. Once David settled into this reality, it became his passion to equip his son and servants for the next phase of this spiritual journey that Israel was on and that he was privileged to be a part of.

Worshipers will soon (if not already) find themselves at the threshing floor through various unexpected events. It will put us in dilemmas that we never thought we would have to face. As a result of these unpredictable circumstances, G-d will compel us to come back to Him with a different perspective. This perspective will be the *first* step in bringing the Body of Christ to the worship experience that YHWH has always intended for us to enjoy with Him. However, I emphasize that it will only be the first of many steps in the journey. I restate that point so that we don't abort the process by thinking that the first step is the journey; it is just the beginning of a process that will bring one of these generations to the place where we will be prepared as a bride adorned for her groom.

There is a place of worship that exceeds the lifespan and knowledge of our present age. It predates David and his generation also. It is a worship that was established prior to the creation of Adam. It is a place I strive to understand and apply to my own worship. Just as David built upon a location that was predetermined, so we are not the owners or authors of this great worship theory. It began within the profundity of YHWH Himself. My commitment and the choice of every believing worshiper today is to receive it and practice it without question or debate. We don't have to understand why G-d desires something to accommodate His desire. As servants of the Most High and subjects of His great kingdom, we are obligated to oblige the King of His every desire so as to maintain our relationship with the kingdom. If we stay on the threshing floor until we get rid of our chaff, we will become a useful grain of wheat valuable for even greater usage.

CHAPTER 5

TRANSITIONING FROM MOUNT GIBEON TO MOUNT ZION

David was only the second king of Israel, so we can only compare his leadership to that of his predecessor, Saul. Still there are marked differences between the two leaders that give tremendous insight into worship and ministry today. In order for the Church and its leaders to make the necessary transitions to move to authentic and significant corporate worship experiences, we must acknowledge the leadership that we have in the Church today. This leadership falls into two major categories: those who are interested in worship and those who are interested in war.

Whether you realize it or not, a Saul or a David is leading every church and ministry. If you have a Saul-type leader, there will be a particular ministry focus and certain things manifest in the ministry. What is most obvious about the Saul leadership personality is that it tends to be focused upon war, conquest, and personal gain. The victory in every battle is related directly back to the leader, and thus, the leadership gains credit and notoriety for its conquests.

When a leader is most concerned with winning battles, every situation tends to be viewed from a win-or-lose perspective.

What's interesting is that Saul was chosen and then anointed; David was anointed long before his public recognition. David was chosen because he was a worshiper, and G-d desired a man after His own heart. Saul was chosen because he had military qualities, and Israel desired a leader to compare to the leaders of other nations. In many cases, our leaders today fall into this competitive mentality where there is a constant comparison and evaluation based upon what someone else is doing. This is so dangerous to leadership because that leader will be driven by the need to conquer for the sake of keeping pace with another church or ministry and not driven by the mandates of the King and His kingdom. Saul quickly moved into disobedience within two years of his reign simply because he was not submissive to the dictates of YHWH via the prophet Samuel.

The other thing that a warrior leader does is create a warring environment within that ministry. I've noticed over the years how so many churches constantly suffer from infighting, inner turmoil, and unnecessary stress, most of the time simply because of a warring leader. As a matter of fact, it is so common that they know no other way to function. The pastor fights against the board, the committees against each other, the choir against ushers, the hospitality group against the pastor's aide group, the deacons against trustees, and so forth. Churches that function like this on a whole are typically led by a warrior. This warring leader is on a mission to subdue, conquer, and win, and it causes everyone in that ministry to function the same way. This was the only concern of Saul throughout his tenure as king. It created wrong motives and inspired jealousy; it weakened his leadership from within and caused G-d to reject him. When the leader has to fight for everything, it is a sign that the leader is not reliant upon G-d.

The other noticeable characteristic about warring leaders is that they are less concerned about worship. When you look at Saul, it is obvious that his worship is ritualistic and not relational. He doesn't worship out of passion and purity, but rather out of protocol and practice. Therefore, his worship is not noted as being preeminent in his life. This is made clear by the fact that Saul did not inquire of the Ark of the Covenant throughout his entire reign as king. He participated in worship ritual, but did not inquire of the Lord. The warrior leader follows the protocol and practices the ritual, but never inquires, in submission, of the will of G-d. Saul's feeble attempt of worship in First Samuel 13 is a clear indication that he only engaged in the ritual to save himself from personal defeat and embarrassment.

The Church has been stifled by leadership that is only concerned with personal gain and credibility. The people are used by the warring leader for conquests that seem spiritual on the outside, but are carnal on the inside and only provide another victory to be recorded on the leader's resume. The warring leader has short-term goals and does not impact the kingdom, leaves no kingdom legacy, and has no succession plan. Such leaders are quickly forgotten because their win-at-any-cost leadership style satisfies only one person and leaves no lasting impression on the large majority of those who serve. Saul is rejected before his death and forgotten after his death. There is no memorial of his leadership and no significant recognition, even though he was the first king of Israel. He won wars and pursued his enemies, but he never became a worshiper, and that ultimately became his demise.

David, on the other hand, was a worshiper from his childhood. He became a warrior by necessity, but as soon as he rested from his enemies, he went back to his first love—that of a worshiper. When David came on the scene, he came as an anointed adolescent worshiper who was already skillful with the harp, his worship instrument. He came to serve and not be served. He came as a support to the kingdom and denied what G-d had already revealed to him about his own destiny just so that there would be no confusion in the kingdom. This is proof that David was not a warrior at heart.

If he was a warrior at heart, he would have contended or strived to assume leadership as soon as he came on the scene. Instead, he chose to wait for the Lord to exalt him, and he was content to function as a servant until that time.

Worshiping leaders have an anointing that far exceeds the present leadership, but because they are unwilling to create chaos and confusion in the kingdom, they will wait on the Lord's timing before making any moves. This is important because David must be recognized as a worshiper and not a warrior. His notoriety in the kingdom comes from serving the king with his worship music first and killing Goliath second. In this way, his victory over Goliath can be attributed not to his handling of the sword, but rather to his relationship with the G-d of Israel.

Once David moved into complete authority over Israel (see 2 Sam. 5:12), he shifted the national focus to that of worship. The next chapter begins with David retrieving the Ark from the house of Abinadab, where it had been for over twenty years, and bringing it into Jerusalem with great celebration. The corresponding Chronicles passage says that they had not inquired of it since the days of Saul, which, in fact, meant that since it was returned to Israel when Samuel was prophet, no one during Saul's tenure had inquired of it. The warring king was not concerned with worship or the Ark. However, as soon as David had opportunity as leader over all of Israel, he brought the nation back to a place of worship and reverence for the Presence.

The worshiping leader is always concerned with bringing the entire congregation back to its original focus: worship. Israel was established for this reason from the days of Abraham straight through to the Mosaic era. Israel was to be the only nation on the Earth who worshiped the true and living G-d. The return to such worship represents YHWH's original intent. The destiny of the worshiping leader is always to bring the people of G-d back to their original purpose.

David's pursuit and desire to have the Ark near for the purpose of worship is, at the same time, significant because it marks the beginning of the transition from the Mosaic era of worship to the Davidic era of worship. It is important to note that this transition is precipitated by David's desire to return to his worshiping posture more than the maintenance of his warrior posture. If he wasn't a worshiper, Israel could have continued as they had in the days of Saul. David's identity as a worshiper was, therefore, instrumental to the direction of Israel as a nation. Whenever the leadership is driven by a desire to worship, it brings a dynamic into play that has limitless implications as to the direction of that ministry. The worshiping leader is now given the liberty to move in realms that were previously inaccessible. Thus, David took this bold step of retrieving the Ark from the house of Abinadab and brought it into the city of David, not realizing that this was the beginning of a national transition that would forever reposition Israel in worship.

However, no transition takes place without complexity. David was a worshiper, but he was still a man, and the worshiping journey that he and Israel embarked on evolved and developed in natural terms into the divine plan of G-d. As David made this aggressive move to bring the Ark into the midst of Jerusalem, his motive was commendable, but his method created a problem.

In the process of bringing the Church to its proper place of worship, we must make sure that our motives, which are noble, don't cause us to disregard the method, which has been previously established. David, in his haste, failed to take the time to investigate the proper way for the Ark to be transported, and it cost him and Israel dearly. Uzzah, according to Scripture lost his life by touching the Ark as it became unstable at Nachon's threshing floor, and this loss was directly related to David's negligence. This tends to be the case even today whenever there is a major transition in the Church. The ones who are involved in the application of the transition take the blows for the leaders who moved hastily and gave them bad information.

David should have taken the time to research how the Ark was to be transported from place to place. This would have saved Uzzah's life as well as spared him and Israel the embarrassment of having death interrupt such a great celebration. This is one of the things that concerns me today about the movements and trends that we see in the Church. Musical fads, worship trends, sanctuary designs, marketing schemes, and worse things that are being done tend to have no scriptural documentation, theological reference point, or doctrinal basis. Yet we implement them and advertise them simply because they seem to have a little glimmer of triumph attached to them. Yet they are not proven through Scripture nor have they been proven through time nor have they been tested universally. David had the right motive—bringing the Ark back among Israel to be reverenced as the place where the Presence dwells—however, the method by which that motive was carried out had fatal consequences.

Still G-d was faithful to His worshiping leader, who more than anything just wanted to move back to a place in his life where he could worship freely in the presence of the Lord. As a result of this faithfulness and David's inquest for understanding, three months later he had the method in place to match the motive. The three months becomes an important point of reference for us today. It was in this time that David allowed the Ark to rest in the house of Obed-Edom until he discovered what to do and how to do it.

During The Worship Center's (TWC) time of transition, we were willing to do nothing but research for a season until we discovered what G-d wanted and how to present it to Him. Most ministries are not willing, under any circumstances, to do this. Yet for a season we trusted G-d to keep the continuity of the congregation from Sunday to Sunday, and we did no other type of service—no Bible study, no special revivals, no anniversaries, no meetings. I encouraged the congregation to do research on the things they had questions about as I did the same from the corporate perspective, and we trusted G-d to bring us to a new place of understanding so that our worship would be authentic, meaningful, and powerful. I took my cue from David in this exact text and did exactly what he did so that I, like he, could get it right. It was risky, but it was worth it. The mission was accomplished shortly after this time of event sabbatical. As a result, just as in David's case, G-d *gave us* what He desired in corporate worship, and we have been following it and continuing to evolve in it ever since.

What David did is what the Church needs to do today. It needs to go back beyond the previous generation of ministry, beyond the last one hundred years; it must go back to the introduction of corporate worship to discover what G-d desires and what has never changed since that time.

David went back to Numbers 4 and the days of Moses, which predated him by about 500 years, to find out how to carry the Ark. He could not have discovered these things from his recent history because, in that history, they either didn't do it properly or they didn't carry it at all. This is the key for this generation. We tend to look back to recent history to attempt to regain our footing, and what we don't realize is that recent history was doing it wrong also. So we can't go to the previous generation or even three or four generations back. We have to go back to the introduction of corporate worship to humanity and start there. That introduction represents the genesis, and the genesis gives you original intent.

I advocate that we have been in error for so long that I can't find a decent example of worship anywhere in the history books. I had to go to the Book of History, the Bible, to get my paradigm straight. It was during this investigation that the Lord showed me Jeremiah 6:16 as a basis for my understanding. He made it clear that the Church was standing at the crossroads attempting to make a choice about its future direction. As I looked at that passage closely, the Lord made it clear that neither of the paths I was focused on were right. The path He wanted me to walk on was so ancient that the path was now grown over with trees and shrubs and was not recognizable to recent generations. In other words, He would have to show me where the path had been since it was so ancient. Then, after showing me the path, He would charge me to have the courage to begin to remove the trees and shrubs and make it a path again for generations to come to walk on. It was at that point that I understood that this journey would be like nothing I had seen or admired in recent history. Just as it was with David, the challenge is: Do it right, or don't do it at all. What will we choose?

The first time David moved the Ark, he did so many things wrong it wasn't funny. However, no one realized it until Uzzah died. Everyone thought everything was just grand. Isn't it amazing how, as long as we have a crowd and noise, we are raising money, and our leadership is intact, we don't have any idea how wrong we are? There is no unction to reexamine our practices while we are experiencing success. But once we experience tragedy, that's when we go desperately looking and searching, often only to save our own reputations. When David marched the Ark in the first time, there were no sacrifices before the Lord, and the Ark was being carried in a new cart, which was only a replication of something the Philistines introduced to Israel. There was no consecration of the Levites and no division among the Levites according to their scriptural responsibilities. Worst of all, a dumb oxen was responsible for the stability of the Ark. How tragic is that? YHWH could not have been more disrespected. Then again, some of the things we see today sure rival it.

With all of this, it was still the mercy of G-d that he only took the life of Uzzah and not the whole camp. Taking Uzzah's life gave David and all of Israel a chance to examine their ways. If G-d had not suddenly and tragically interrupted this celebration, David would have thought that the method he was using was pleasing to G-d. So we must be grateful when our practices are rejected by Heaven through failure; it is our chance to go back and get it right.

Three months later, when David began the process again, he made it clear that they had not researched or sought instruction on the proper way to transition the Ark and that is why they had suffered failure (see 1 Chron. 15:12-15). This time the Levites were sanctified, they functioned according to their division and order outlined in the books of Moses, the Ark was secured upon their shoulders, and sacrifices were made to the Lord. As a result of this reverence for the Presence, YHWH was pleased, and the Ark was transitioned successfully. This marked the beginning of a new paradigm in worship, because it was during this celebration that music was introduced to the corporate worship experience before the Ark of the Presence.

David's paradigm of worship was now clearly defined for all of Israel. David himself danced before the Lord as the music was played, and the people rejoiced. David was not only the king, but he was also the worship leader. Unlike in the days of Moses, David was demonstrative, exuberant, and expressive about his worship. The solemn, quiet, and fearful worship paradigm was being removed. Never before had there been music or dancing or singing before the Presence. David was changing worship eternally on Earth. After the Ark was successfully transitioned, it was not placed in the Mosaic tabernacle structure. To do that would be like putting new wine in old wine skins. David was audacious when he placed the Ark in a tent that he had previously prepared for it. This was a deliberate move away from the only tradition Israel had ever known, and this shift was divinely ordered and endorsed by YHWH because it was prophetic.

The move to the tent, which would later be known as David's tabernacle (see Amos 9:11), is the only era of worship G-d has said He will restore in the last days. He will not restore the tabernacle of Moses or Solomon's temple or any of our recent eras and trends, but the prophetic nature and implications of David's tabernacle will be restored so that the Church's Christ-centered worship will be authentic and pleasing to Him. This is the pivotal characteristic of this revelation in worship. What David was divinely inspired to institute is what we ought to be drawing from to shape and develop our worship today. No one challenged David's move—not the elders of Israel or the Levites—even though they had just researched the entire Mosaic paradigm. Somehow G-d anointed David to make this move without any religious opposition or controversy. To me, this is a clear indication of a divinely mandated change.

However, it pays to examine what preceded this dramatic shift. Prior to David's actions, there was indifference toward the Ark and the Presence, indifference toward worship in general, a diminished expectation toward G-d, and self-centered leadership. The earthly setting was perfect for this new era to be introduced without resistance. The people were tired of war and needed rest, and they welcomed worship because it reestablished the preeminence of the Sabbath and rest. As it was then, so it is today. We will return to G-d's original intent because the time is right, the era is right, and the atmosphere is right.

This entire process began because David desired a dwelling place for the Ark due to the fact that he dwelt in a great house of cedar. As worshipers, our focus must return to "the place where the Presence dwells" and not just places for us to dwell. When that becomes our driving force and passion, I believe G-d will meet that desire with wisdom and revelation that will continue to take worship to newer heights. Israel was enticed by YHWH Himself upon their departure from Egypt, in that He would dwell in their midst, and they would be distinguished by that context above all other nations. Somehow today that paradigm has been absolved in light of our desire to be rich, famous, and important in the eyes of the world. We have bought into the world's success measurements and have forgotten that the conclusion of the matter is to fear G-d and keep His commandments, for this is the whole duty of people. Whether we abound or are abased in this life, it is secondary to His pleasure. Our one desire should be to know that His Presence is nigh and to live graciously in that splendor.

So David placed the Ark in the tent he had prepared for it and then established a new precedent of worship. He assigned Asaph and the Levites to full-time twenty-four-hour worship. He commanded them to make noise in celebration and commemoration of the Presence all day and all night without ceasing. This looked like the fire that never went out in the days of Aaron, but now it was the responsibility of worshipers to keep the fire burning internally in their spirits of worship before the Lord. This was a remarkable departure from the Mosaic paradigm. The Mosaic tabernacle was quiet, pragmatic, and solemn. The Davidic tabernacle was musical, noisy, and energetic. The difference was so significant that there was really no resemblance of one to the other. Music was in David's tabernacle what incense was in the Mosaic tabernacle.

He also set a new standard by breaking the protocol of going from Outer Court to Inner Court before entering the Most Holy Place. Essentially, it was just the one dimension that David focused on. This was prophetic in nature since there was no Outer Court and Inner Court. The concept is that the worshiper is given direct access to YHWH with no preconditions. This is reminiscent of Adam in the Garden and the Father's original intent of fellowship with His creation without hindrances or barriers. This means that David was advocating a face-to-face worship experience. YHWH was nigh. In the same way, the woman at the well in Samaria desired a greater understanding of worship from Jesus, and she ended up with a face-to-face experience with the Messiah. David's paradigm suggests that the day is coming when there will be no veil between the created and the Creator. This could only become the reality once the blood of Jesus was shed. Yet David functioned as if that blood had already been shed in that he only had one dimension of worship in his tabernacle and not the three dimensions noted in the Mosaic tabernacle. I will extract more from this tabernacle concept later.

Another notable difference in this Davidic worship is that everyone who participated in the worship left with a tangible blessing (see

1 Chron. 16:1-3). David was intent on making sure that every man, woman, and child departed from this worship experience with the tangible fruit of their worship experience. Unlike the Mosaic experience, where you came with your offering and left empty-handed, this experience was different. David changed the perception of worship and offerings. Today we still see the Mosaic paradigm practiced more than anything else. The people come, and they have to sacrifice finances for everything they receive. It has gotten so bad that prophets make you pay for prophecies, and demanding apostles and so-called fathers make you pay to be a son or daughter. Even in the natural, the sons and daughters don't pay for anything until they are of age and the parents have finished sowing into their futures. I've seen people close to me sow into their spiritual fathers, and then when they get into a jam, those same fathers do not write them a big check to help them out. And then I often wonder to myself, if these fathers where so dynamic and anointed, why do the sons and daughters struggle so much just to make it while their fathers are striving and prospering. I always thought that if my father prospered, that automatically meant that I would prosper since everything that my father has is mine.

Nevertheless, David set a new standard for who must be blessed after worshiping, and that is the worshiper, not just the leader. Every person goes away with something tangible or useful. Ministry must provide significant deposits into the people so that their lives are as prosperous as the leaders' lives. David supplied every worshiper with some practical benefits for their participation. The bread (need), the meat (want) and cake (desires) could be enjoyed immediately. Ministry cannot just promise the invisible blessings to the worshiper while the leader is going home with the visible benefits. They must go home with something practical as a result of their corporate worship experience.

It is at this point that the transition began in earnest from Mount Gibeon to Mount Zion. Since David had now set the Ark in the tent that he had prepared for it, there was a dilemma within David as to how he should go forward with the corporate worship. So David did something that we all experience to some degree when we are making thoughtful transitions. We tend to leave the old tepidly. Scripture makes it clear that David did not abandon the Mosaic worship completely (see 1 Chron. 16:37-42). He sent Zadok the priest and his brothers to Gibeon to sacrifice and worship according to the Law of the Lord, which cannot be abolished. So as David was moving away from what Israel had known for the last 500 years, he struggled with how to satisfy what was and what is.

This is true for all spiritual transitions as well as natural. Psychologically, emotionally, and mentally, we always struggle with the process. Whether it is moving on or how to move on, it can be challenging to do it effectively, especially when there is no precedent. Throughout my own personal Christian experience, I have been through several dramatic and significant transitions. It was only after several experiences that I began to document and analyze what precipitated these changes and then recognize my naivety while going through them. Through this process, I could perceive with greater clarity how to minimize the consequences of doing it wrongly.

I can recall transitioning from a wholly Baptist experience of worship to a Pentecostal one. I can remember transitioning from sitting in a pew to being called out to receive a word or prayer. I can remember being motionless (sleepy) to clapping and dancing during worship. I remember going from a completely inauthentic human-made structure of church governance to a scriptural leadership paradigm. I've recently undergone some major shifts in worship at TWC that include the way we receive the gifts, the elimination of annual celebrations, moving from a choir to Levites that minister before the Lord, a two-hour service to a timeless worship experience, and last but not in any way least, acquiring space to accommodate a growing congregation versus building a house to facilitate the Presence.

So what we see with David is not necessarily surprising. However, what becomes difficult to reconcile over a period of time is worshiping in a tradition versus worshiping in the Presence. When Zadok and his brothers went to Mount Gibeon, they were very much aware of the fact that beyond the veil there was a Most Holy Place that was void of the Ark, which represented the location that the tangible presence of the Almighty dwells. Eventually, worshiping without the Ark will become an empty experience.

This is where so many churches and parishioners are today. They are beginning to recognize that the only thing that makes worship authentic is the presence of YHWH, and if He is absent, the worship is an unsatisfying experience. Many churches will hold to their traditions no matter what, but they will, in the process, render themselves irrelevant. Then others will come up with new innovative and creative ways to entertain the congregations, only to divert the parishioners away from the realization that YHWH is still absent. Still others will boldly lay claim to their significance as it relates to G-d and worship and subtly suggest there is no need for G-d as long as they are present. Since the world is full of those who are gullible, ignorant people, we will have this until Jesus comes and rectifies that Himself.

While the priests go through their rituals at Mount Gibeon without the presence of the Ark, it was a sign of a dying worship paradigm. It wouldn't be long before the Mosaic tabernacle was retired. Its retirement, however, was not an abolishment of the concept that it introduced as a genesis of the corporate worship experience. As I stated in the Introduction, the Lord made it clear to me that today's earthly worship experience gleans from each era, and the Mosaic era has much to offer. That is why the writer of Hebrews refers to this earthly (Mosaic) tabernacle design as a copy of the true tabernacle that was erected without human hands (see Heb. 8:2). This means we cannot ignore or abolish what Moses did as it represented something far greater than just an era that could be ignored or tossed aside just because we now have the New Testament Holy Spirit paradigm.

If that was the case, there should not be such a specific reference to it in Hebrews with a direct association to the significance of the work of Christ in light of that tabernacle.

Most of my critics misinterpret these statements as suggesting that the *ekklesia* is not the temple of the Holy Spirit. To say or suggest that would be to contradict Scripture, and I am not saying that. What I am doing is making a distinction between what the corporate worship experiences should look like and what has become worship in our churches today. My desire is to do this in a way that does not harm the indwelling of the Holy Spirit in the believer for the purposes of personal worship, empowerment, and continuity with the larger Body of Christ. What we must reconcile at some point is the fact that the corporate gathering will continue until Jesus comes. They will lose momentum, denominational dominance will dwindle, foolishness in the pulpit will be challenged more and more, and what we have done in the past will continue to mutate into the latest trend, but the corporate gathering will continue. If it continues in so-called church buildings or facilities of any sort, my concern is: What will be the significant attention-grabber in that setting? Whether you gather in someone's home or a coffee shop or a large hall, who will the eyes of the people be trained on, and what will they do with that spiritual attention? If we do not deal with this issue, we have simply painted the brown horse with zebra stripes. We'll fool a few ignorant people, but over time everyone will know it is still a horse.

David only initiated this transition, but he didn't live to see the fulfillment of it. When David died, the process was passed on to his son, Solomon, for completion. Solomon assumed the throne with the architectural framework, spiritual order, and the money for the temple. David made sure that the continuity of the transition would not be broken because his inexperienced son was unprepared. He provided every conceivable resource to ensure his success. Yet with all of this in place, Solomon began his reign with the same dilemma that David ended his with: experiencing YHWH in authentic worship.

I am intrigued when I look at Second Chronicles 1:3-4 because I wonder to myself how difficult it must be to find yourself in leadership of a nation of more than a million people and not know how to experience authentic worship. Solomon went to the high place at Gibeon because it was the tradition of Israel, but the Ark was not there, for *"David had brought up the ark...to the place David had prepared for it..."* (2 Chron. 1:4). So Solomon was caught between what was and what is just like his dad. That night Solomon prayed himself out of paradox and into the new era of worship. G-d was merciful and directed him to build the temple, thus signifying the end of the Mosaic era. At that point, Scripture gives no indication that Solomon returned to the high place at Gibeon for the purpose of seeking the Lord.

The transition was completed when Solomon finished the temple and brought all of the articles from the Mosaic tabernacle and introduced them into the temple era (see 2 Chron. 5:1-5). It's almost like the Mosaic was dissolved into the temple era. It wasn't forgotten or discarded, but brought down with all of the furnishings so as to honor where it all began, while moving forward to what now was. This is why I believe each era has some authentic shadowy concepts that must be understood in order for corporate worship to return to YHWH's original intent.

We can't just throw away corporate worship because it has evolved away from what G-d originally intended. We can't just abolish anything without acknowledging what should follow and how it should serve the same purpose, but better. I cannot agree with those who are simply so dissatisfied with what the *ekklesia* has become that they believe we have to trash it without remedy. Christ above all is the head of the Church (not one of us), and He was and is fully prepared to deal with what we have become over time. Yes, we have pagan roots and practices, dead churches, dysfunctional leadership, corrupt government, and celebrity spokespeople, but Christ is still the head of the Church.

My prayer, like so many of you who are reading this book, is that we would come to a place of revelation about YHWH, the Son of God, and the Holy Spirit and yield to their will. This to me is the greatest shalom that can be experienced while on Earth. To know what pleases the Father and to facilitate it individually and corporately is the highest joy the creation could ever know.

CHAPTER 6

THE RISE AND FALL OF THE TEMPLE

The era that encompasses the time that Israel's worship dignity was recognized by the temple Solomon built on behalf of his father David is far too great to cover in this chapter. However, the concept behind what that era meant to Israel's corporate worship and what it means to ours today can be conveyed clearly. Within this era, the goal remained the same: to further the discovery of what worship should look like today in light of the preceding eras. There are things in the temple era that can be discarded and are no longer applicable, but there are other things that continue to express what G-d wants when we come together to worship Him.

I begin with how this era came about and what precipitated the transition. I need to reiterate how each transition in hindsight was predictable, and some of the same things that existed during the transition from the Mosaic tabernacle to Solomon's temple can be seen in modern Christianity.

The primary instigation for the temple era came from David (see 2 Sam. 7). David rested from his enemies and had time to reminisce about the thing he loved the most: worship. These moments of reflection brought about a creative desire for the Ark of the Covenant to be placed in a more glorious and prestigious décor than that of a tent. David's comparison between his dwelling place and the place where the Presence dwelt caused him to want to build a house for the Lord. YHWH made it clear through the prophet Nathan that, throughout Israel's history, He had never desired or requested that anyone build Him a house. This for me is a clear sign that G-d's psychological connotation upon His people has always been that He desires to be viewed as mobile, spontaneous, unpredictable, and uncontainable. The fixed structure changes that imagery.

Now the other part of David's motive is exposed in Second Samuel 7, to the degree that G-d makes it clear that David's legacy will not be sustained via a physical structure, but rather by a spiritual heritage. This is seen by the context of the prophetic word that Nathan brings, which ends with the assurances found in verse 16. *"And your house and your kingdom shall be established forever before you. Your throne shall be established forever."* What this suggests is that this part of David's motivation to build came out of his own personal insecurity about how he would be remembered by Israel. This tends to be the issue today with modern ministry. Leaders build structures and establish fellowships or conferences as a memorial to their leadership so that their obituaries will be impressive and memorable. This is typically born out their own subtle yet obvious insecurity about what they have done in ministry. That is why the structures we see today speak more about the leader than they do about the leader's G-d. G-d knew what was in David's heart regarding his legacy, so He comforted him with the words of Nathan's prophecy and also gave him information and direction as to how this great temple would be built.

With this in mind, G-d still did not prohibit the building of the temple, which intrigues me. This meant that what David desired to do was acceptable. Why? This is the next obvious question, and the answers bring us clarity about the changing of that era of worship.

The simplistic reason for the shift from mobile to stable is that Israel was no longer a nomadic nation. The Mosaic tabernacle was convenient for the mobility of the nation. Now that Israel has become established in a territory, there was no need for a mobile tabernacle. But it went deeper than that. The tabernacle remained mobile for all those years following the conquering of the land by Joshua and the defending of the land by other leaders and kings because no one knew where its permanent location should be. Which of the tribes should "own" or be responsible for such an awesome national relic? The Levites did not inherit any land, so the likely candidates could not claim they were due, though the tabernacle was their responsibility. If one tribe had that privilege, it would eventually create envy by the others, so that wouldn't work. So the tabernacle remained mobile because no one knew the "location" that it should be set in permanently.

So when David came along and wanted to set the temple up as a permanent worship center for all of Israel, G-d didn't reject it because His desire was to dwell in the midst of Israel, and now the only thing left to establish would be the location. This would mean that the transition from the Mosaic era to the temple era of worship was sanctioned by YHWH. Having a temple in the midst of the nation would facilitate the promise that G-d was with them always and that they never had to travel outside of their land for corporate worship.

The temple then became the focal point of the national life of Israel, and you can see it as you read through the Old Testament. Chronologically, everything from the time of the building of the temple to the beginning of the New Testament is related to the reverence and worship or lack thereof of YHWH via this temple, along with its location. I interpret that this physical location, which was representative of Israel's corporate worship, was of paramount importance to the spiritual life of this nation. Though some of our modern Christian voices would refute this statement, I believe the physical location still has critical value in the corporate worship experience today. That being said, it is in no way fulfilling its responsibility of facilitating worship as it was originally designed to do, and

I will talk more about that in another chapter, but it is nonetheless critical to the identity of the organism called the *ekklesia*. At least at this point, there is an understanding as to how this transition came about and what purposes it would serve for the nation.

The rise of the temple era and its prominence throughout the Old Testament should be directly related to David and his desire to see the Ark and the place of worship reverenced properly by Israel. So when we look at the greatness of Solomon's temple and the excellence of worship that was exhibited in its inception, we should see it through the eyes of a worshiper who wanted nothing more than to *"dwell in the house of the Lord all the days of my life, to behold the beauty of the Lord and to inquire in His temple"* (Ps. 27:4). If we see the temple era this way and if we see the way the Lord accepted what David attempted to establish as a continuation of the Mosaic worship tradition, we will be less critical of what corporate worship has become. True, the temple will not retain its spiritual luster over the long run, and the era will run its course, but the concept and establishment of a location where the Presence will dwell must be contemplated.

What we are missing today in the modern Christian experience is the concept that the Presence can have a dwelling place in the midst of the people even as the Holy Spirit dwells within us. This does two things. It allows us to walk and live this life with the indwelling of G-d's presence via the Holy Spirit, and it allows us to experience the Presence of our Father when we gather corporately. This also helps to eliminate the real skepticism that exists because we don't really believe that our neighbors are filled with or baptized by the Holy Spirit since we often see them in their weakness and in their strength.

Though Solomon is given a full array of instructions from his father David, he still seems to be tentative after David's death. So Solomon's first act as leader of Israel is to seek the Lord for direction. I admire Solomon for not just assuming that since his father gave him the green light to build that he should just go ahead and do it without inquiring of the Lord. Certainly, if nothing else, the timing of the project needed to be ascertained directly from Heaven.

When Solomon pursued this prayer, he took all of Israel with him to the high place at Mount Gibeon to worship at the tabernacle Moses had built in the wilderness. At the same time, the Bible so subtly but obviously states that the Ark of the Covenant was not there (see 2 Chron. 1:3-4). In fact, at that point, it was still in the tent that David had prepared for it when he brought it up from Kirjath-jearim. It is fascinating to me to see Solomon and all of the leadership going to worship without the Presence. I imagine that there was some confusion or dilemma on the part of Solomon as he was betwixt worshiping based upon Israel's tradition versus where the Presence was now.

This has to be the major dilemma of the modern corporate worship experience. The Church today seems to be perplexed between tradition and what G-d is doing. We tend to hang on too long. We tend to move away, but then come right back. We tend to change superficially while remaining traditional in essence. We are in the same position that Solomon was in. Yet in Solomon's case, G-d clearly directed him away from this tabernacle when He spoke to him by releasing him to fulfill the promise made to David regarding His dwelling place.

There is a real need for the renovation of worship today just as in Solomon's day. We need to throw away, get rid of, dump or however you want to label it; we need to demolish the present worship traditions so that we can renovate according to what G-d Himself desires. Modern worship needs an overhaul. We need to do what they do on the makeover reality shows. I saw the television program called "What Not to Wear," and in it they approach a prospect with the opportunity to get a makeover if the person is willing to get rid of the clothing he or she presently possesses. If only the Church would take G-d's offer to get rid of all that we possess in order to be made better by what He picks and chooses for us.

I believe the shaking that the Church will experience and is experiencing right now is designed to compel us to change. Some renovations aren't done by choice; they are done by imposition. As the worship in some churches becomes less and less relevant, less compelling for the parishioners, less convincing and convicting, the changes will come by force, or some churches will just go out of business (and we've been seeing that already).

When Solomon went to Mount Gibeon to worship and sacrifice in the Mosaic tabernacle, he was faced with a glaring reality; he could not worship in two places. To do that would create confusion for all of Israel. Even today, we try to appease the young and the old. We try to be contemporary and traditional at the same time. We have a traditional service at one hour and then a contemporary service at another. We don't realize that ultimately it creates confusion for the church. They are worshiping in two places spiritually. The Bible says that Solomon sought the Lord with a thousand burnt offerings, so as to get YHWH's attention. It's almost like Solomon was saying, "I'm going to pray my way out of this paradox." When Solomon received his answer to prayer, he was able to walk in wisdom and knowledge, and he was able to execute the plan that his father, David, had left for him to accomplish. If we pray and seek the Lord for as long as it takes, we will get His *desire* and *design* for worship in this season before Christ's return.

Second Chronicles 2–5 documents from the preparation through to the completion of the temple by Solomon. When he was finished with the building of the temple, something interesting happened during the preparations for the dedication. The Bible says that they brought up the silver and gold and all of the furnishings that David had dedicated (see 2 Chron. 5:1-5). Then it says that they brought the Ark, *the tabernacle of meeting*, and all the furnishings that were in the tabernacle. Did you catch that? They brought Moses' tabernacle and placed it within the temple. They didn't throw it away, they didn't leave it where it was, they didn't set it up next to or behind the tabernacle; instead, they sort of *dissolved* it into that era. This is a phenomenal revelation because we in the modern Church still don't know how to reconcile a previous era in light of our present revelation without just tossing it in the garbage.

When I shifted TWC into the celebration of the Passover, some thought I had lost my mind. Questions arose as to whether or not it was replacing the Communion and as to whether or not I was taking us back to something that the Lord told us to stop, as if I was breaking some New Testament Church rule by celebrating it. However, while teaching the importance and significance of the Passover, I was reminded by Scripture that Jesus Himself celebrated it. It was and is not a covenant, but a memorial, and that is why the Lamb of G-d celebrated the Passover Himself.

I believe somehow that our disconnection from our Hebraic roots has created this terrible misunderstanding and misinterpretation of how we are to reconcile the Jewish practices of the past to the Jewish practices of the present. The New Testament Church has become this separate and distinct entity that only associates with our Jewish roots through the use of Old Testament stories and not the assimilation to the Hebrews from a heritage perspective. This disconnect is the reason why we have basically rendered the Old Testament as a shadow of things revealed in the New Testament, and after that, it is useless for our present interpretations or worship. This obviously is not true of scholarship, but it is definitely true of the contemporary expression of Christianity.

Solomon had the wisdom to dissolve the Mosaic era into the temple era without impediment. It made sense to him not to leave it on a mountain to corrode, rust, and wear away with time. For Solomon, the patterns were the same, the dimensions were the same, the tapestry and colors were the same, the purpose for which it existed was the same; the only real difference was mobility versus stability.

In one sense, Solomon allowed the Mosaic to maintain its dignity even in its retirement. This is why I believe G-d has me writing this book. Again, it is so that we can examine these eras and extract from each one valuable components that we should have never discarded. If we are able to capture what G-d wanted and still wants today in worship from these eras, we can begin to move back to His original intent for corporate worship.

Now the grand procession of the Ark commences with great significance on the awesomeness of the Presence. There is great sacrifice, sanctification, and singing to commemorate the Ark of the Presence. Today we only seem to have the singing in place in most churches. We don't give the full complement of honor to the Lord's presence anymore. We have discounted the sacrifice and the sanctification as not being as important as in the days of David and Solomon. Imagine offerings that could not be numbered! The people brought so much and Solomon prepared so much that they lost count. We're always keeping count of how much we are giving, almost like a hostage note for Heaven so that we can remind G-d later that we gave a certain amount and now He owes us for what we have done.

We really don't understand offerings nowadays because the church leadership has so manipulated and mangled this sacred part of worship until it is not sacred anymore. I can remember in times past being in a church service of a profound and notable speaker. The word the speaker delivered was a blessing, the service had impact, and then the speaker "raised the offering." That single act undermined everything that came before it. I can remember watching as the time taken for the offering exceeded the time taken to minister to people at the altar, and in some cases, it matched the time spent for the message. I've experienced preachers "locking the doors" and not allowing anyone to leave during the offering. I've experienced people saying, "I'm going to wait on G-d's money!" and many other types of manipulation surrounding what should be viewed as sacred. I heard one mega-preacher say, "Don't bring me no five dollar bills."

When he said that, I put my offering back in my pocket, and he got nothing from me.

It has so impacted me and my ministry that at TWC we no longer pass a plate, have people march around the church to give, or anything like that. The teaching on tithing, giving, and offering has been done periodically from a totally different perspective. As a result, when we receive the Lord's offering, there is no specific mention of it at all. As a matter of fact, we have made it our practice that, at any time during the worship experience, you can bring your gift and put it on the altar; that's it! We make it clear in our handouts that you should do this on your own without any coercion or manipulation from the pulpit. From the time we began that practice to the time of the writing of this book, the offerings have steadily increased year after year fifteen to twenty-five percent. (This increase was maintained even during our recent recession.) I will never ever attempt to get people to give what they did not determine to give on their own before they left their houses. If they rob G-d or cheat Him with their offerings, it's between them and G-d. Yet at the same time, I am instilling within the saints a belief that I trust them to do what is right in the sight of the Lord.

The importance and significance of bringing the Lord a sacrifice will never be diminished by foolish church practices, but the way that many leaders have manipulated people to give is something they will be judged for. David gave instruction during his reign, and Solomon maintained the practice, and the people gave more than could be counted. So what was the great motivation for giving? The simple answer is: the Presence. Whenever the Presence is present, you don't have to do anything to get people to give. They give because the Presence of the Almighty compels them. When the Presence is absent, you have to create an alternative reason to motivate, inspire, or manipulate giving, but when the Presence is manifest, people are spiritually compelled to give willingly and cheerfully.

So what we see today does not match what Solomon experienced that day in worship. People give to get today. They sow only to reap. They don't sow to be obedient or give because they honor the shekinah and want to secure His presence for generations to come. Today's givers are looking for something in return. So the true sacrifice is missing in our worship today, which causes the worship to be inauthentic.

Then there is the issue of *sanctification*. For the most part, it is a foreign term unless you are presently enrolled in Bible school. The term is used in biblical education often, and there may even be a class on the subject. But the issue of sanctification as it relates to worship is unfamiliar to this generation. Sanctification is not part of the vocabulary of the contemporary Church. To speak of such a thing is old fashioned. Nowadays, we hide behind the blood of Jesus, the cross, and goose-bumps as our validation for living any old kind of way. Nothing matters anymore since we have the blood. However, I am always arrested by the words of Paul in Romans 6:1-2, *"...Shall we continue in sin that grace may abound? Certainly not!..."* Yes, G-d forbid we ignore the reality of contrary lifestyles while claiming that the blood has taken care of it.

The truth is that G-d demanded of Moses and Aaron sanctification in order to participate in His worship. The Hebrew description of the word is clear. It means "the process or result of being made holy." *Sanctification* is the necessary component of being set aside for G-d's exclusive use. It means that the vessel is holy and pure and usable for holy service. Moses and the Levites went through a separation and a setting apart, and He demands the same of this generation, whether it will adhere to it or not. We are to be in the world and not of the world. We are to be salt to Earth, and if salt loses its savor, what will the Earth be salted with? We are to be light in dark places, not darkness in dark places. Yet this generation insists upon doing "church" without sanctification, and it will cost them dearly.

A tolerant society prides itself upon inclusion and acceptance without criteria or standards. Historically no society, organization, or community can maintain its virtues under such circumstances. It is a recipe for implosion and disaster. The Body of Christ can be described biblically as having already been sanctified by the blood of the Lamb. Unfortunately, that understanding has done one of two things. It has released the callous to live carelessly because their sanctification is already secured, or it imposes an obligation to live up to the standard that sanctification in Christ has secured for them. The greater concern, however, is that the modern Church experience makes no mention of sanctification as a tenet of our faith, and therefore, today's Christians live in ignorance of their holiness obligation. Either way you look at it, the contemporary Church is put at great risk for effective and acceptable worship with negligence so great in this area.

Solomon was well aware of his father's mistakes while attempting to bring the Ark into Jerusalem the first time. One of the biggest mistakes he made at that time was not sanctifying the Levites who would do the service of handling the most holy piece of furniture in Israel's history. That negligence cost Uzzah his life. The second time David moved the Ark, everybody involved went through a sanctification process. To be useful in this area, we must possess an acceptance of what G-d mandates and a willingness to comply.

So the sanctification, sacrifice, and singing preceded the shekinah falling in the temple and will precede the shekinah being manifest in our worship as well. With these things in mind, there are still some additional facets of the actual worship experience that bring clarity to what is expected of us in worship today.

I must highlight that the level of worship experienced by Solomon and the Levitical priesthood was accomplished by an unusual "one accord-ness." They were able to fine-tune their worship in such a way that YHWH only received one sound from the temple. To help us to understand what may have happened at that time, it will pay for us to understand how sound is emitted. In the simplest context, sound travels in waves. The waves move atoms by virtue of pressure. When music and singing is taking place at the same time, typically they are moving through the atmosphere at different rates of time, which is defined by frequencies. This is necessary for us to not only hear sound, but distinguish the diversity of sounds.

Since G-d is not limited as we are to pressure, atmosphere, and frequencies, He must have been distinguishing the unique spiritual continuity of the commitment and desire of the worshipers to give Him perfection in both instrument and voice. When YHWH received what was being emitted from the sanctuary, it made one sound due to its spiritual quality more than its natural qualities. Spiritual continuity and a commitment to perfection bring the worshipers into one accord; when that sound and type of worship is presented before the throne, it takes on a "one-ness" quality in the spirit realm. One purpose, one intention, and one desire by the worshipers translates into one sound before the Father.

The other thing that must be highlighted is that, at the time of this supernatural outpouring of Adonai's presence in the form of the cloud, the priests could not minister. This is a picture of third-dimension worship in its fullness. As the Ark was set in its place, and the priests honored the glory of YHWH, He came in, in His fullness, and took up residence in the Most Holy Place. What happened at that point was that there was no need for human influence at that level of worship. This is the awesome plateau that I envision the Church arising to in days to come—a place of no human influence. When I see the Church emerging in worship, I see it driven not by the typical human motivations and instigation, but by the raw and unveiled presence of YHWH.

The third dimension of worship is a place where there is no music provided by a human. There is no pastoral encouragement, no apostolic oversight, no prophetic impartation, no singing inspiration, but just the glory of the Presence that Israel experienced throughout their days in the wilderness. In this place of worship, everyone bows, including the priests and the Levites. In our context, that would be a difficult thing for those who worship based upon the recognition of their status; however, this is what third-dimension worship is about. It is about Him and not about us. In this dimension, the bishop bows right next to the janitor, and the executive secretary next to the organist, and the bus driver right next to the apostle. When the Church is able to embrace this wholeheartedly, then we will see the manifest glory like they experienced in the temple era.

This marked the beginning of the temple era. What you will notice chronologically in the Old Testament is that from this point on everything in the spiritual life of Israel was centered on the temple. Whether it was regarding the refurbishing, the reverence of worship, the destruction, or the rebuilding of it, it all focused on Israel's life around this place where the Presence dwelt. What I gain from this is not that the focus was on the temple per say. It was actually what the temple housed, which was the Ark of the Covenant. In modern Christianity, there is a lot of talk about the needlessness of the church building and how it has become a sign of paganism and how it no longer offers anything worthwhile to the saints, and to this degree I agree. If the physical building that is referred to as the church or the place where the church meets does not house the Presence, indeed it is no longer relevant. However, if the building where the church meets is indeed the house of the Lord and it houses the Presence, then the location is very significant.

In the days of Solomon's temple, Israel had an assurance as to where they could find YHWH. For them, it was most significant to know that He dwelt between the cherubim, as nine or so Scriptures assure us. Since that was the case, G-d was essentially keeping His promise to Israel that He would dwell among them, and Israel knew His location at all times. No other nation could claim the Presence or His actual earthy location. In using this terminology, I do not suggest in any way that G-d ceased to be omnipresent. Still, for the sake of dissimilarity, Israel had a unique distinction among all the nations of the Earth. The New Testament Church has difficulty reconciling this reality in the age of the Holy Spirit. However, if the New Testament Church could translate this concept into our modern theology, we would understand that the Holy Spirit dwells within the saint as the Father dwells in the midst of His people.

What is valuable about this concept to me is that, in the case of the unsaved or unregenerate coming into our worship experiences, they would first be confronted by the Presence of YHWH and not just the presence of people. This would create a distinct challenge for the human spirit in that it would have to reject the very presence of the Lord to leave that place unsaved rather than just reject our sermons, songs, and praises as inauthentic and unconvincing. Jesus said, *"No one can come to Me unless the Father who sent Me draws him..."* (John 6:44). Yet in our present setup, the only thing drawing in most cases is our human effort. This has to change for one main reason: it is not working!

So what we need to do is not discard the church building for the coffee shop or the living room; we need to redesign, renovate, and realign the church building to be transformed into the house of YHWH. We need to design the interior according to what is prescribed specifically in Scripture so that the Presence can come and remain in our midst forever. We need to take bold and assertive steps to divorce ourselves from the pagan practices and traditions of historical people and move in faith back to what will indeed satisfy the Father.

During the dedication worship, Solomon prayed an interesting prayer which is recorded in Second Chronicles 6. In this prayer, he mentioned over and over that if Israel or any foreigner found himself in trouble or difficulty of any sort, that they should pray toward the temple (the place where the Presence dwelt), and Solomon asked over and over that G-d would hear them and deliver them because they prayed toward this place. Solomon petitioned G-d in this prayer to *"Hear from heaven Your dwelling place"* over and over again (2 Chron. 6:21). It is a phenomenal request on Solomon's part. At the close of this prayer, the Bible says that the glory of the Lord filled the temple again, and the priests were not able to enter to minister. The second glorious manifestation, with fire falling, invoked worship and praise again by all the people, and then something amazing happened, again! The king and the people started bringing offerings again. This is what the glorious presence of the Lord will do if we set everything in order that He desires. When He shows Himself in this magnitude, we don't have to say or do anything; His presence alone is enough to provoke everyone to sacrificial action.

Now once Solomon accomplished all that he was to do for the house of the Lord (see 2 Chron. 7:11), then the Lord appeared to him in the night. What happened next should cause us to rethink the latest trend of holding corporate worship in just any old location. YHWH said that He had heard Solomon's prayer *and* that He had chosen *this place* for *Himself* as a house of sacrifice (worship). He further stated that His eyes would be open and His ears attentive to prayer made in *that place* (see 2 Chron. 7:15). So the location that was designed and consecrated and that housed the actual Ark of the Covenant was not like any other location when it came to corporate worship. It was peculiar in that it was the place that YHWH designated as special to Himself. If we accept this as an essential theological component of our worship experience today, we will not discard it because it has been perverted. Instead, we will defend it as if it has redeeming value for worshipers yet to come.

While there is so much criticism of the Church today, really that criticism should be leveled at the leadership. It is really the leadership that has caused the Church to look the way it does today. This is why, in the verses that follow, the balance of what the Father has to say is directed at Solomon and the leaders who would come after him. G-d made it clear that if the leadership turned away and forsook Him, the entire nation would suffer, including the land and the temple.

So what we see today is a direct result of leadership that has forsaken the truth, the commandments, and the Word of G-d and has basically turned toward the god of money and other worldly desires. They have melded these carnal passions into their theology and now promote it as some new and creative way of viewing G-d and the Scriptures, but in fact it is nothing more than their attempt to justify their perversions while remaining or seeming religious. As a result, the Lord has rejected the leadership, the people, the lands, and His house, and we marvel today at the desolation of the modern Church.

What I marveled at in looking through the balance of the Old Testament is that we see no further glorious manifestations of this magnitude as a result of worship. What we see at the beginning of Solomon's temple is the last time we see it. Is it that the shekinah never left from that point on? I'm not so sure that would be a completely sufficient answer. However, what concerns me most is the comparison I find in our Christian history as in the days following Solomon's era in the temple. Rehoboam, his son, two generations from David, had already begun to move away from the standards that David had established for worship. By the time we get to the fifth year of his reign, the house of the Lord was plundered (see 2 Chron. 12:9). This is amazing from a generational standpoint. Yet we see the same in our Christian history, that by the time of most of Paul's writing to the Church in various locations, they had already begun to suffer from bad leadership and erroneous doctrines.

It is at this point that we begin to see this ebb and flow of Israel, its leadership, and its worship. We see this rise and fall of the temple depending on who is leading the kingdom. Kings such as Asa, Jehoshaphat, Jehoiada, Joash, and Hezekiah came to power and mandated cleanups and renovations of the temple. They had to remove strange things from this holy place and tear down things that had been raised up (high places) in defiance of the G-d of Israel. Jehoiada appointed leadership for the temple, Joash repaired and then forsook the temple, and Hezekiah cleansed the temple and reestablished worship—all because their predecessors had forsaken the ways of David and ignored the place of the Presence.

It is incumbent upon leadership today to go back to the ancient paths (see Jer. 6:16) and find the good way and walk in it. But just as in Jeremiah's day, leadership tends to suffer from a bad combination of arrogance and ignorance. When G-d stopped me in my path, when I was complaining about the people as if they were the problem, that is exactly what He said to me. It shocked me when He said, what if they are not the problem; what if you are the problem? I was so convinced that I had it all in order that I didn't even consider that I could have been contributing to the problems in the local church, much less the Body of Christ.

The rise and fall of the temple until the close of Second Chronicles is typified by the kings who either did what was right in their own eyes or what was right in the eyes of the Lord by walking in the ways of their father David. In other words, David got the revelation about worship and passed it down to his son, Solomon. David had a heart after G-d. David saw something different about the glory of the Lord and prophetically instituted a worship paradigm that would last until the return of Christ. Yet those who came after David, in most cases, forsook what he had established or did not even investigate with any determination what he had introduced to corporate worship.

Here we are, thousands of years after David, writing books, marketing worship paradigms, and introducing trends that have little to do with the principles that David implemented during his short era. Here we are undermining what G-d said He would be sensitive to if we honored Him. Here we are thousands of years later telling people it is okay to leave the location where corporate worship takes place because it will never get back to its original intent, and we are just as good worshiping in the coffee house. Why have we done this? Well it is very simple; we, like David's grandchildren, have no real acquaintance to him, so it is easy to deny what he established. We write it off as Old Testament. We are the Body of Christ, and we are born-again believers in whom the Holy Spirit dwells. The only problem I have with this is that we are not manifesting what the saints manifested in the days following the ascension, and our worship pales in comparison to the worship that Israel experienced in the days of David and Solomon. I pray that our arrogance doesn't hold us hostage to our ignorance and cause us to continue in the modern trends of worship too much longer.

My confidence is that Jesus is and will always be the head of His Church, and He has already begun the process of conforming us into His image and will not cease until He and the Father are indeed satisfied. We might think we are the kings of the Church because of our present day notoriety, but we aren't in charge of anything when the King of kings makes His wishes known.

Finally, when you look at the final thirteen verses of the Book of Second Chronicles, you can get a very vivid picture of where we are today in the Body of Christ. Though there are gatherings in pockets of the world that are experiencing true worship, the vast majority of the Church is suffering from leadership that has forsaken truth and the withdrawal of the glory of G-d from our sanctuaries. He is allowing the enemy to come in and plunder everything that we have so that His house can remain desolate until it has enjoyed its Sabbaths. Then out of the most unpredictable venue, He will raise up a voice and a people to bring His house back to His original intent.

CHAPTER 7

THE FRANCHISING OF THE JEWISH TEMPLE

The era of corporate worship that is characterized by the gathering in a synagogue is technically still in existence today. It was fascinating and maybe somewhat confusing to me when the Lord included this era in the four major eras of worship He spoke to me that day in my office. In all of my Christian upbringing, I had never viewed the synagogue era as a season of worship. Quite frankly, being raised in a Protestant environment that was purely Gentile, I had subtly viewed anything Jewish as separate, weird, and to some small degree foolish. Though a host of my Sunday school lessons often mentioned the synagogue, it was always in a negative light because of what Jesus did while He was in them. To characterize the synagogue era as a worship era demanded research and understanding.

I began by looking up the Greek words that are used for synagogue in the New Testament as well as the Hebrew terminology and when it first appears in the Bible. The Greek and Hebrew interpret the word the same—"a place of assembly" used by Jewish communities primarily for public worship and instruction. The origin of the synagogue is virtually impossible to trace. However, it is believed by most scholars that synagogues became the alternative assembly for worshipers who were deprived of temple worship in Jerusalem. This means that synagogues could have developed as a result of Babylonian captivity and were a necessity as a result of the Roman victory over the Jews in AD 70. They became vital to the community because they served as the place where the Law of Moses was interpreted as well as Jewish manners, customs, and beliefs.

If this origin is true, then that means that the synagogue concept of corporate worship was not initiated or authorized by G-d. It simply evolved out of the necessity of having a gathering place for Jews who were either in captivity or just found themselves so far from Jerusalem and the temple that they needed to establish some type of religious precinct for prayer and Bible study. If we assume that this is the case, and we can do so because there is no scriptural precedent that establishes the synagogue, then it is easy to see how the synagogue became such a controversial and eventually loathed institution. I say this because the earliest accounts of Jesus in the synagogue are all an affront to what was happening within them at the time.

It is easy to deduce what was happening in these synagogues by Jesus' interactions with the leadership of the synagogues and the people who gathered there. I categorize several of these issues here for the sake of comparison to our present-day church gatherings. It will help us to see how the modern Church really serves as a type of synagogue more than it does a corporate worship environment. The purpose here is not purely critical, but it is more so an acknowledgment that it will be impossible for corporate worship to fulfill the Father's purposes if we do not change the venue (or setting) that we are attempting to accomplish these goals in. At the same time, many progressive, exciting, and thriving churches will not even consider these options because of the intoxication of their apparent success. An honest look at the following synagogue issues will serve as a catalyst for any congregation to make the necessary adjustments to remain relevant in this season of corporate worship.

I begin by looking early on in the Book of Mark, where there is a clear sign that the synagogue must have been absent of authoritative teaching (see Mark 1:21-22). I notice that the people's response to Jesus' teaching was astonishment. We can extract the obvious from this observation and deduce that the typical synagogue teaching was boring, redundant, or just uninformative and uninspiring. So when Jesus came into the synagogue, teaching with authority, there was an immediate comparison between Him and the teaching of the scribes. Though the leaders of that institution had great influence and were considered powerful by all standards, their ministry obviously lacked *spiritual* command, authenticity, and relevancy.

Matthew 4:23 marks the first New Testament reference to the synagogue, and it is a very interesting one. It says that Jesus began *"teaching in **their** synagogues,"* which is an interesting statement to start it off with. It almost sounds as if there was some assumption of ownership that was subliminally attached to the synagogue. This association was more than likely based upon who ran and controlled them. Yet Jesus began there because He knew that it was the best vehicle to use in order to begin to correct the mismanagement of the faith that had so permeated Israel since and before the Babylonian captivity. If Israel would ever get delivered from their rabbi-centered faith, Jesus as a rabbi would have to confront it directly. Therefore, He began to teach and preach in their synagogues.

What I love about the onset of the ministry of Jesus is that He began by preaching the Gospel of the kingdom. This in and of itself is strange language for the synagogue setting. Typically, the synagogue setting simply dealt with the Law of Moses and its interpretation, along with the readings from the prophets. But here came Jesus teaching and preaching about something that no one else was speaking about while using the same source material, the Torah. This reminds me so much of what we are seeing today in the modern

Church experience. Though we are very creative with our sermons in America (in particular), and we are highly skilled in biblical knowledge and understanding, many messages we hear today are redundant. They have different seasonings, but most preachers and teachers are gleaning from the same pool of worldview information, and it shapes their messages into the same broad generalities. This is what makes so many of our churches boring, redundant, uninformative, and uninspiring. Jesus came not only teaching and preaching something different, but He demonstrated something different. The Scriptures state that, along with the message of the kingdom, He manifested healing and deliverance. As a result of using the synagogue setting, His fame went out throughout all Syria, and He did even more demonstrative ministry.

To a large degree, ministry today looks amazingly like the synagogue ministry of Jesus' day. We have these franchises of the main denominational headquarters located all over the world. We boast of our ability to franchise our ministries in different areas, and because of that boasting, these ministries begin to subliminally look like they belong to us personally. Then we control them and run them as if they are the epitome of authenticity and no one else has the truth that we have, yet those who attend the franchises week after week have a different opinion. Their opinion in most cases is the same as the opinion of those who heard Jesus speak for the first time. Parishioners are uninspired by our redundant worship services.

Every year these ministries do the same thing in a different location or with a different theme, but always on the same day in the calendar year. Weekly services follow the same format and are very predictable. We have secured new and exciting orators who are charismatic and can ensure us that the crowds will be wowed; however, we are paying a lot of preachers a lot of money these days, and yet there is little manifestation of the power of G-d. If we are able to accept these assessments, then we will be open to change. If we are unwilling to acknowledge these truths, then we put ourselves in the same predicament as the synagogue of Jesus' day. Just as Jesus exposed their fragility and fraudulence, He will do the same to today's congregations that have erred from their original purpose.

The synagogue also exhibited a strong hierarchal structure to it. In Mark 5:22, a common term is used for Jairus when he came to beg Jesus to come see about his sick daughter. The term used is described in Greek as "chief, director" (*archisunagogos*) of the synagogue. Thus the suggestion here is that there were others under him, and it was by this structure that the synagogues were run.

What's interesting about this story is that, as seemingly great and important as Jairus was in the synagogue, he realized that his ministry had no power to heal. In light of this impotence, he humbled himself and came and fell at the feet of Jesus to beg of Him a healing for his daughter. Jesus demonstrated His desire not only to heal the girl, but to win the entire synagogue over to Himself by this healing. Certainly after a healing like that, the ruler of the synagogue would give glory to Jesus and thus authenticate His ministry.

This shift in our present-day leadership is as necessary now as it was then. We have impotent leadership in churches all around the world who are simply functioning in ministry based upon hierarchy and structures that are human-made and have been sustained through the assumption of authority with no manifestation of power. If this type of humility could be achieved in our present ministry setting and changes could be enacted, we could see an authentic move of YHWH in this generation—not just the kind that is drummed up by marketing expertise.

Another strange connotation about the synagogue is that rabbinic responsibilities were misinterpreted. In Luke 13:10, there is a story about Jesus teaching in a synagogue when He noticed a woman who had a sickness that didn't allow her to stand up straight. The Scripture states that she had been in this condition for eighteen years, which suggest that people in this area probably knew of her and her condition. When Jesus spoke healing to her and laid His hands on her, she was healed, and it was the Sabbath. Now the "ruler" of the synagogue didn't like being upstaged in general, but this took it over the top. So he couldn't restrain himself, and he yelled out to Jesus a misinterpretation of the Law. He stated that healing should take place on any day other than the Sabbath day since healing was interpreted as work in his mind.

Now what concerns me is that the ruler of the synagogue should have known that the Law of Moses clearly stated that the priest profanes the Sabbath by his service in the tabernacle, and he is allowed to. What this means is that the ruler had misinterpreted his role of service to be that of a cushy position of being served and not a position of service to those in need at "any and all" times.

What does this look like today? It looks like what we see today as the misinterpretation of the role of the bishop, pastor, prophet, or whatever titled spiritual leader we see today in the Church. They have so misinterpreted their role that now it seems that the whole ministry is designed around serving them, their needs, and their agendas. How did we get so far off the mark that we no longer labor on behalf of the people? It is very simple; we have set up these little self-governed, self-controlled entities that function totally independently of the kingdom of Heaven and have structures that are non-biblical. As a result, the functionality of the average church mimics what we see in the synagogue in Scripture at the time of Jesus' ministry.

To further exacerbate the point, if we take a close look at the ruler of the temple in this story, it is unnerving to think that he would speak this way to Jesus in public. The way he makes his statement, boldly and with no apology, clearly indicates that this guy was in control, and he wasn't in the least bit intimidated by Jesus or the miracle that just took place in the face of the congregation. He was determined that the level of arrogance and control that he was used to functioning at was in no way going to be diminished because of Jesus. Still, his hypocrisy was exposed in the way that Jesus responded by highlighting the inconsistency of his argument.

So we conclude that the synagogues of that day and many churches today are filled with leadership who function out of arrogance, control, and hypocrisy. At the same time, the broken, wounded, and hurting congregations continue to suffer from insufficient ministry and often go home the same as when they came. The expectation of a miracle or a supernatural occurrence is no longer present. Congregations today, like the ones in Jesus' day, are forced to be content with the way things are because there are basically no alternatives. Every synagogue in Jesus' day functioned from the same basic format.

A further problem existed in the synagogue that is similar in our churches today. This issue is found in the story of the man born blind receiving his sight in John 9. In the account, Jesus again was found healing someone on the Sabbath, and the Pharisees were upset about this act and launched an investigation into who did the act. As a part of the investigation, the parents were called in to undermine the fact that their son was born blind, so as to discredit the miracle Jesus had performed. When the parents were challenged by the Pharisees, verse 22 says something very interesting. It states that the parents were fearful to give a straightforward answer because they feared that they would be excommunicated from the synagogue! Again, we not only see the control that the Pharisees and temple rulers exhibited, but also the fear that was imputed upon the congregants by the leadership.

I can barely find a member nowadays who does not have a similar horror story about experiences at a local church. As a matter of fact, I have my own horror stories about the way I have been treated by some of my pastors in the same context. It is amazing how Jesus stated in John 2 that "His house" shall be called a house of prayer for all people, yet we find reasons to put people out of His house whenever they don't agree or line up with our human-made rules and regulations or whenever they seem to challenge our control of the church. So many people in churches have relationships with their pastors and leadership that are purely based upon fear and intimidation rather than love and appreciation. So the issue of expulsion still exists today in a lot of churches, and this ought not to be.

Let's look further at some of the other issues that the synagogue had in the days of Christ and see if there are any more noticeable comparisons to today's Church environment.

In John 8:37-59 and Matthew 3:7-9, the Jewish leadership expressed a theological argument that was refuted by Jesus. They said repeatedly that they had Abraham as their father as a security hallmark of their faith. This hereditary connection apparently gave them privilege that superseded the theology that Jesus was bearing witness to. If this theological opinion prevailed in the synagogues, then that would be a clear sign that the synagogue was a place of bad theology. This meant that, on a regular basis, they were teaching that the Jews enjoyed a beneficial position by physical heritage that allowed them to practice any habit or contrary discipline and still remain connected to the faith by virtue of their natural connection to Abraham. When Jesus confronted this issue in John 8, He argued that if you do not do the works of Abraham, you cannot claim a spiritual connection to Abraham. What the Pharisees and others believed was bad theology that was largely based upon the convenience of application and not the whole truth of the faith.

This kind of thing is also prevalent today. Bad theology is the reason we have empty churches, broken and hurt people, disillusioned leadership, and weak and powerless congregations. There is a deep need in this day for leadership to invest time in researching the Word of G-d for applicable revelation as well as for the reordering of how we function within the corporate worship setting. Bad theology is very simply an inaccurate study of G-d. It is one that is based upon assumptions of previous theological opinion. It is one that is based upon misinterpretation of Scripture because the wrong foundation is being used for the interpretation. It is one that is built upon contemporary thought or based upon an individual's carnal worldviews. It is one that is not balanced by supporting and corroborating Scripture. It is verses extracted from their context. It is Scripture interpreted with no Hebraic support. It is someone approaching Scripture with a preconceived notion. It is the absence of the interpretation of the Holy Spirit. The synagogue suffered from bad theology because the Pharisees, Sadducees, and scribes had a stronghold on that environment and could not in any way be challenged by an outsider or attendee. Many of our churches today function from the same general protocol.

Leadership today would truly benefit from not making assumptions based upon the interpretation of the past. Some theological truths remain consistent no matter what, and I am not attempting to tamper with that which is obviously unchanging. However, there are a lot of practices that are still in place today that are based upon misinterpretations of the past. There are a lot of belief systems that need to be included in a healthy and productive discussion so that we can come to some universal conclusions about what G-d is saying today and how we need to proceed in light of these revelations.

Churches have become so confusing that, moving from one to another, the theological opinions and suggestions are so dramatically different that an outsider is quick to abandon the process of finding G-d via the local assembly. The bad theology has to cease, and recalibration must begin if we are to have any type of impact on this world via our worship experiences.

Additionally, the synagogue of Jesus' day had become a place of hypocrisy, pride, and showmanship. This is typical of any religious environment that is absent of the Presence. In Matthew 6:2,5, Jesus made an observation that those who do a charitable deed or those who stand and pray in the synagogues are really hypocrites because they do the deed or act for public recognition. When you look at both of these Scriptures, you notice that Jesus made a direct indictment on the synagogue in both cases, and in both cases He called the people who did these things in the synagogues, hypocrites. In other words, this religious environment had evolved so far away from its original purposes that it was now conveniently supporting self-glorification.

Today it seems that the self-glorification has gone to an entirely new level. Glorification and glamorization of the flesh has a day, a special service time; it's promoted with flyers and radio announcements and invitations with high ticket prices. We can't preach or teach without it, we surely can't sing without it, and any noteworthy thing that is done in today's Church environment has to be acknowledged in a fleshly way. Jesus calls it hypocrisy. With this in mind, I am becoming increasingly skeptical of what we are calling revivals today. Some of what we are calling a move of G-d can easily be called a move of the flesh. If you take the main personality away from some of these settings, the entire worship experience changes. We have evolved just as the synagogue did, away from original purpose. The local assembly is no longer just a place of worship, prayer, and the study of the Word of G-d. It is no longer a place where the Holy Spirit is the leader and takes precedent over every other agenda. The original purpose of the Church never included the special acknowledgment of those who did special works on behalf of the ministry. But now we name pews and halls after people because they donated a certain amount of money to the church. This should not be! Nothing should be done in G-d's house for human recognition. Every act of kindness or spiritual practice should be done for the sake of furthering the kingdom of G-d, and the participants should be content to receive the rewards for their service when they meet their Master in Glory.

In the same context, Jesus also dealt with the pride and showmanship that existed in the synagogues at that time. He spoke in Matthew 23:1-6 about the burdens that the scribes and Pharisees put on others that they themselves refused to lift a finger to do, all the while seeking only to do the things that made themselves look good in the eyes of people. Jesus highlighted their pride in the way they dressed to impress and added extra religious connotation to their outfits to seem more spiritual than the rest. Then He emphasized that, in the case of the synagogue and feast, they were quick to take the most prominent seats so as to be recognized by people.

I can't help but see the parallels in today's Church environments. We suffer from so much pride and showmanship until it is widely accepted and expected. The more well known you are, the bigger the entourage, the grander the entrance, and the higher the fees. Most of our leadership today who practice these things would like us to believe that it's warranted. Somehow I don't believe you need a bodyguard to go to a worship service, but you can go on vacation or to the supermarket by yourself. Furthermore, if the angels can't protect you at a church service, what good are they?

The pride and showmanship has just diminished the integrity and respect of the ministry across the board. Yet these issues are not new. They existed thousands of years ago and will continue to exist as long as there are prideful men and women on the Earth. Jesus addressed these issues in His day, and we ought to address them in ours. We are given a clear picture of the fundamental problems with the synagogue situation and what needed to be done to expose and adjust it. It was gutsy for Jesus to take on pride and hypocrisy in His day and it will take just as much guts to expose and deal with it effectively in our day. I highlight these things here because noting them is essential to our recognition of why we have lost power and relevance in the Church and how we can begin to reposition ourselves so that we can be useful for the kingdom again.

The task that Jesus undertook in His day is almost unheard of in our day. Typically when we see someone making these types of observations, they are written off as comments from an angry, disconnected conservative who is not only frustrated with his own ministry, but uses criticism as a platform for creating an audience. Jesus, however, understood the value of being critical, while not forgetting His ultimate goal of bringing about a transformation via the religious organization that was presently in place. He was fully aware of their inability to make drastic changes, but He created accountability by highlighting their errors and giving them an opportunity to repent.

The observations made throughout this book can and should be viewed as critical, but not for the sake of being critical or creating a platform on the foundation of other ministry's miscues. The real motive is to create a sincere dialogue about what the Body of Christ has been left on the Earth to represent and how to better accomplish the goals of the Head of the Church. He longs to see us move back to His original intent and, just as in His day, deny the errors of our tradition for the sake of authenticity.

In Matthew 15:1-9, Jesus was in the midst of highlighting the inconsistencies of the scribes and Pharisees, while attempting to get them to look at the proper application of the Word of G-d and not the traditions of their elders. The manipulation and exploitation they practiced in the synagogues was done in the name of tradition, yet it was clearly taking advantage of the congregation to their benefit. The manipulation of Scripture for the financial benefit of the leadership is not new. It was a problem in Jesus' day, also. The manipulation of Scripture is probably the biggest problem we have in the modern Church. It is not so much that the leadership is uneducated or undereducated; it is the fact that some Scriptures do not serve the selfish motives that they have contrived in their hearts, so they have to twist the Word to make it fit their alternative purpose. At the same time, the pew is vulnerable and less educated and can easily be manipulated by a charismatic leader, and therefore, they tend to follow whatever they are told without question.

If that is not the case, most large groups are simply manipulated and exploited by the traditions of that group. Jesus confronted this manipulation with a proper interpretation of the word and an accurate interpretation of their motives. The denominational structures of our day have largely fallen under this same context. The shear longevity of these groups seems to serve as the biggest platform for their practices being unquestionable. Their traditions are long-standing, and their founders and patriarchs are saintly and untouchable, so the manipulation can only be dealt with by martyrdom. This is essentially what Jesus suffered at the hands of those who saw Him as a threat to their systems of control. The traditions of people, the standards of dead elders, and the influence of a large group of people who have been successful over time are a hard thing to come up against. Typically, they have the mechanics in place to render the opposing voice irrelevant or unreliable. However, when the challenge is against the proper interpretation of truth and motives, I believe, just as in Jesus' day, the jury (audience) will begin to distinguish between the power of an organization and the power of G-d to back up His truth with tangible, indisputable, undeniable evidence. This was the deciding factor in Jesus' day, and I believe it will be the distinction in our day.

Look again at the Pharisees in John 9, as they seemed to function in desperation trying to convince a healed man that Jesus could not be trusted or glorified for healing his blinded eyes. They pressed him about his condition, and then they pressed his parents for clarity on whether or not he was truly born blind. The parents redirected them back to the young man to speak for himself. They tried again to discredit Jesus and described Him as a sinner. Finally, the young man said to them, *"Whether He is a sinner or not I do not know. One thing I do know: that though I was blind, now I see"* (John 9:25).

This will be the ultimate verdict imposed upon the local churches, denominations, and religious institutions that are attempting to keep people in ignorance and bondage. Those who have experienced something more than a sermon, a church service, or religious traditions will begin to vouch for the reality of the supernatural move of G-d. At the same time, they will denounce without fear the systems of manipulation and control that have kept them from experiencing His Presence personally all of these years. Just as in the case of the Pharisees in John 9, I believe this present Church leadership is feverishly attempting to hold on to their last bit of influence as a tidal wave of powerful experiences are occurring just a ways offshore. There are churches that are seemingly thriving in the synagogue system, and just as in the days of Jesus, they are able to propagate the image of confidence and control. However, just as Jesus created a revolution by His words and deeds, quietly there are revelations being released in the Earth and manifestations to substantiate them that will render the old systems irrelevant in a short time.

The main problem with the synagogue system as it has been observed and compared to today's churches is that they are mostly void of authentic worship and consecration. Remember that this setting is dramatically different from that of the temple. The main difference is that there is no Most Holy Place. The other differences are obvious in that there is no resemblance at all to the temple because they were not set up to do what the temple did. With this in mind, it is easy to see how the synagogues eventually would not even facilitate a decent spiritual experience. The entire design and setup did not evoke worship and consecration. So the issue of worship was truly on the back burner when people came into a synagogue in Jesus' day.

If the backdrop of our present church design and setup is the same as the synagogue, then it would be impossible to facilitate authentic worship in our settings also. So though there are ministries who are sincerely attempting to facilitate an authentic worship experience, they will constantly be frustrated with the inconsistency of their efforts because the essentials are missing. The future of worship was not tied to the synagogue in Jesus' day and will not be tied to our churches in our day. However, just as Jesus used this venue to declare that there was something better available, the local church and church organizations will be the venues used to declare that something better is available to those who desire an authentic worship experience that is tied to the Presence in the Most Holy Place.

What the Pharisees, Sadducees, and rulers of the synagogues failed to recognize was that Jesus had a message that, when fully exposed, would completely undermine their religious structure. They underestimated the power of His message and the temperament of the people. Jesus' message, when unwrapped, put people in a radically different spiritual position than their messages. Once this message was received, the people no longer needed what they were offering. They also underestimated the temperament of the people. They were under such strong self-delusion that they were blind to the people's disposition toward them. So while they were continuing their posturing and game playing, people had already determined in their minds that they were ready for an alternative to what every synagogue was offering.

This present day trend is visible to me in settings other than the Church as well. Our recent history is showing us that the status quo is functioning like they have in the past while the temperament of its constituents is completely shifted. I see the trend when I look at what's happening in Thailand among people who are typically submissive to their government, but are now willing to spill their own blood at the gate of the prime minister. I see it in Iran, where an entire subculture is surfacing with a martyrdom-type commitment to change. I see it in Lebanon and Syria and many Arabian countries that are attempting to suppress the external influences on their people to no avail. I see it in India, where a new middle class is being formed, and alongside this new opportunity is a disconnection from the traditional strongholds of the past. I saw it in the U.S. in 2008 with the election of President Barack Obama. The Republican base seemed to be completely unaware of the subculture that used a different form of communication than they did and that was driven by a different set of values. In this same way, there are tidal waves that are a ways offshore that are gaining momentum in the open ocean and will be moving far too fast when they hit shore for any type of preventative measures. Places like Myanmar, Saudi Arabia, Nepal,

Zimbabwe, Barundi, Bangledesh, Laos, Cambodia, and Mexico just to name a few, will begin to see the wave soon.

When the religious rulers of Jesus' day attempted to quash the news of His body's disappearance after the resurrection with a few shekels of silver, it was a dreadful miscalculation on their part. I remember preaching a message one Resurrection Day called "A Tsunami Called the Resurrection." I recall using this reference in that message when I stated, "You cannot stop a tsunami with an umbrella!" What these stoic denominations and religious tradition-alists are not aware of is that things have already changed. They do their surveys annually and read their reports in their conferences and still don't discern the data. Even many of our more sophisti-cated and advanced groups are missing the important point that you can't approach spiritual data with an intellectual and scientific matrix for response. What the Church is facing is that the future of worship is going to be indelibly tied to the origin of worship, which means we must go back, way back, to go forward. Unfortunately, most paradigms for worship today are so deeply undergirded by a contemporary worldview that the quest for answers is tainted before the journey begins.

The future of worship is going to be as religion-shattering as John the Baptist's ministry was shortly before the arrival of the Christ. He looked different, he talked differently, he used a different venue, yet he completely fulfilled something that had been spoken of some seven hundred years prior to his arrival. The ministry of John the Baptist in a sense went back to grasp forgotten truths and used them to move forward and prepare the way for Christ. John's ministry was viewed as strange and unconventional; however, it chronically filled a void in that particular spiritual environment that only a revolu-tionary shift could have accomplished.

What's coming will only look different to those who have forgot-ten what the ancient Scriptures said would be coming at this time. However, because of the misinterpretation or former interpretation of some of these Scriptures, we have not reexamined them to discover what the Lord is saying today. Or in some cases, we are just too arrogant to believe that we could be wrong and that YHWH could be doing something new that humbles us and causes us to completely submit to His will. Whatever the reasons may be, what I see coming and what I am describing in this book will indeed fill a void that has been created and maintained by this present religious system. Though the system seems secure and intact today, in a moment of revelation and exposure, it will all dissipate without a trace.

To some degree, it is horrifying to see a tsunami on the horizon and not be able to get everyone out of harm's way. To another degree, it is unfortunate that we have not interpreted even the most obvious history with the honesty that causes us to recognize that the recession of the sea is a sure sign that something unprecedented is about to happen. The religious environment in the days of John and Jesus was a *déjà vu* of several other periods of time in Israel's history. Yet each generation tends to view history as things that they or the fathers lived through and not things that happened so long ago that only an astute researcher is able to harness the information and connect the dots. One of the main reasons that it will be difficult for terrorists to achieve another 9/11 is because the information-gathering gurus are now able to connect events that in the past were imperceptible. This new way of deducing should be enacted by the Church so that we can become like the sons of Issachar and discern the times and know what we ought to do.

The synagogue era produced such religious protocol and arrogance that it was no longer about worship, prayer, or the study and proper interpretation of Scripture. What should have been a sincere spiritual setting was now turned into a self-serving impious monopoly on G-d. This type of manipulation creates a climate that those who are imposing and crafting this religious treason are in no way prepared to handle when it reaches fulfillment. I strongly believe we are living in the days of this fulfillment.

The antipathy toward Christ and the cynicism toward the Church and Christianity are at an all-time high. The people who we most dearly need to reach are infected the most. From one corner of the globe to the other, churches are failing to inspire and invoke a need to know YHWH through Christ and thus follow His example to live a successful life. They spend more time trying to satisfy themselves than the Lord's agenda. They are making themselves irrelevant in this world at an alarmingly fast pace. This generation is so far removed from having a relationship with G-d that, for most people in the twenty-first century, it is a foreign concept. Synagogue churches will fade from the scene like remembering telephone numbers. One day, we had a bunch of most dialed, most important numbers in our heads, and then without really recognizing it, we started speed dialing through a tiny computer chip, and we can't date it, but we ceased to remember numbers any longer. One day in the not too distant future, people will suddenly wake up and (speaking of a church building) will say, "What is that building for?"

Though this day will be dreadful and unexpected for many, like a tsunami, I'm anticipating and expecting it with great preparation, and I am heading to higher ground. For me and hopefully for you, because you're reading this book, higher ground will be positioning your worship and walk of faith in such a way that not only will you be unaffected, but you will be able to rescue those who ignored the facts. My expectation and excitement is centered on the fact that this is what the Body of Christ is supposed to be in the Earth. We are supposed to have answers to questions before they are asked. We are supposed to have light in areas where the light has never shown. We are to salt this bland Earth with substance, sanity, and sanctity. We are supposed to be the envy of all nations.

This must be viewed as a golden opportunity for the Church of Jesus Christ. We are in a John the Baptist moment. We need to speak differently, look differently, and supply a different venue. We must become preoccupied with preparing the world for the return of

Christ. This is a most unusual time in the history of humankind, and we of all people have been chosen to be alive during this time; what a privilege and an honor! We who believe that there is something more must be willing to break protocol and undermine 500-year traditions if they are not scriptural. We must do this because we have researched and discerned Israel's biblical history, and we are aware that this season is special and spectacular.

I firmly believe Jesus remains the head of the Church and is giving us this revelation and spiritual climate to facilitate spiritual combustion, a perfect storm, a once-in-a-lifetime total eclipse of the sun, an unrepeatable sequence of events that comes along once every 500 years. When the Church abandons its old and irrelevant habits and embraces a new era of worship, it will mean salvation to the world.

The synagogue era, as I have researched it, did not produce much in the way of fulfillment of the purposes of worship. Overall, the era set religion on a course that it is still struggling to get off of today. It allowed things into the religious environment that became toxic and debilitating. However, it facilitated a necessary era of religion that assisted in introducing the ministry of John and consequently Jesus of Nazareth. So I don't despise what the synagogue was in that time; however, I've learned from that time and apply it to this time to give me perspective on what is about to happen and what I should be doing to prepare for it.

CHAPTER 8

THE FOUNDATION OF SANCTUARY WORSHIP

There was no greater worshiper in the Old Testament for me than David. His worship was passionate and personal, but also prophetic and profound. His pursuit of worship should be the inspiration of every worshiper today. He created a picture of what sanctuary worship looks like and how to maintain it. Holding to his precedent would serve the Church well today.

Sanctuary worship for us today comes by virtue of a few congruent spiritual components that need to be understood in their context. The first thing that must be understood about this era of worship is that it is unique from all of the other periods because we worship in the era in which Christ has already died for the sins of the world. No other era engaged in worship in this context. In each of the previous eras, the corporate worship stood on unsure ground because the worshipers did not have the guarantee or confidence to know for sure that their worship would be accepted.

Prior to Christ, it was always a wait-and-see experience. Will YHWH answer by fire? Will He give us a sign of acceptance? Will Adonai be merciful in light of our sin? On several occasions, the children of Israel said, in essence, to Moses, "You go and speak to Him, lest His anger burn against us!" Old Testament worship was always characterized by a few instances of the Lord not accepting what was offered. The picture of this goes back as far as Cain and Abel. However, that context has been removed from the equation since the blood of Jesus has been shed on our behalf. We know that the blood was accepted once and for all on behalf of all of human-kind and has provided access to the Father through faith and trust in Christ the Lamb of G-d. With this reality as a component of sanctuary worship, we are a part of the only era that has been given guaranteed access to the Father through worship.

The second component that must be considered is the active participation of the Holy Spirit within the temple (body) of the wor-shiper. Whereas prior to the coming of the Holy Spirit the worshipers had to go to a location where they would have an interaction with the Spirit of G-d, now the Holy Spirit has been given as a guarantor to the saints to aid and enable them in their personal and corporate worship experiences. This means that even when I am away from the physical sanctuary, I can still engage in *personal* worship in another location as needed or as prompted by the unction of the internally dwelling Holy Spirit. The other eras of worship did not have this as a component of their corporate or personal worship experience.

Now when people come to the *corporate* worship experience, they could or should have been engaged in a personal worship experience at home or in their car as they traveled. So when they enter the sanctuary to join with other saints in the corporate worship of the Father, it is a unique environment because nowhere else in the community can they find an edifice set aside exclusively for worship, a day set aside completely for worship, and a gathering of people who possess the same internal power (*exousia*) to worship all in one space. The worshipers now enter into the tangible Presence having already engaged with the Holy Spirit on an intimate level, and they commence to worship on a level that is potentially explosive every time it occurs.

Due to the internal working of the Holy Spirit, the saints can leave this environment and continue to have the Holy Spirit minister to them about the things that were said and done in the sanctuary. This means that over the next six days the Holy Spirit can remind them of the word that was ministered or embellish the word so that they can continue to glean from it or give them the opportunity to share that same word with someone who may not have had the privilege of being in that worship experience. In other words, the Holy Spirit keeps the corporate experience alive within us many days after the Sabbath.

The third and most powerful reality of sanctuary worship I will elaborate on more extensively later. However, the main point of this third component is that the sanctuary era is the only era that has given the saint unrestricted access to the Most Holy Place where the Presence dwells. In the tabernacle era, the Most Holy Place was veiled and could only be entered into by Moses or Aaron based upon the occasion. It was designed to prohibit unrestricted access by anyone to YHWH's presence because of sin. Even when Moses entered in, a complete preparation and following of protocol was necessary. Ceremonial cleansing and sanctification took place each and every time. Even then, Moses entered in trembling at the awesomeness of the Presence and the experience. Accordingly, in the temple era there was an equally demanding preparation for anyone who did the annual service in the Most Holy Place.

The synagogue era, which overlaps partially the temple era, had no Most Holy Place. The Most Holy Place was exclusive to the temple, and therefore, when you went to the synagogue, you did not have to worry about going *into* the presence of YHWH because the Presence was absent from that setting. This setting was conducive for prayer and discussion of the Torah.

So none of the eras have given the believer unrestricted access to the Presence like the sanctuary era does. The sanctuary era is punctuated by the death of Jesus Christ on the cross of Calvary. It was at the point of His death that, according to Matthew 27:51, the veil in the temple was rent in two, thus opening spiritually and naturally a way into the Most Holy Place. Once Jesus' blood satisfied the Father's eternal requirements for sin, the barrier that the veil represented was removed, and thus, the next era of worshipers could (by virtue of the blood) go directly into the Father's presence and worship Him. Thus the sanctuary era began with this event.

Sanctuary worship is all about being in the Presence for a face-to-face encounter like the one the Samaritan woman had with Jesus at the well. Sanctuary worship brings us back to YHWH's original intent when He placed Adam in the Garden and then met Him regularly at *"the cool of the day"* for face-to-face fellowship, unrestricted and uninhibited. This type of worship yields confidence, stability, and resolution to the worshiper. Things that have been misunderstood for an entire lifetime can be answered and resolved in this kind of interaction. This type of worship is not an event that can be contained, scheduled, or limited to a two-hours-and-fifteen-minutes service. On the contrary, it is the type of experience that it is hard to pull someone away from because it is so addictive and soul-satisfying.

Though we live in the era of sanctuary worship, most churches and Christians do not experience these things simply because most church environments are stuck in a synagogue-type worship experience. As a result, many Christians are in no way experiencing the fullness of YHWH in their corporate worship experiences, and they are unable to manifest the kingdom of G-d in their daily lives. Just as Jesus came during the temple/synagogue era and had to introduce the kingdom of G-d to them, it is the same today. The messages that accurately describe the kingdom and our participation in it are few and far in between. Most of the messages we hear today are simply about surviving as a Christian in this corrupt and evil world. They are all about holding on and hanging in there; they are weak and make the hearer weaker and keep the Church in a deficient position in the Earth. These messages are a clear sign that we are not walking in the reality of the sanctuary era. The sanctuary yields the type of information that puts the receiver of such illumination in the driver's seat calling the shots. It makes them superior and not inferior. It places them in headship and not tail-ship. After receiving information in the sanctuary, you are above only and never beneath. You can't even think defeat, and even what looks like a defeat is really victory in the making.

David was the catalyst for sanctuary worship, and though David was an Old Testament figure, he was prophetic in his embracing of the future of worship. In Psalm 27:4-6, David made it clear that there is *"one thing"* that serves as a preeminent and paramount desire, and it would be the driving force (*"I seek"*) in his life eternally. He said that dwelling, beholding, and inquiring were his motivations during worship, each of which creates a precedent for what sanctuary worship must be composed of.

David's one desire was described in threefold fashion. Beginning with *dwelling,* the word in Hebrew (*yashab*) means "to sit down, to remain, to settle, or to marry." He said that, more than anything else, he desired to sit down, settle in, and be married to the house of the Lord for the rest of his life. This represents a deep passion for the *location* that is called the Lord's house. This passion has been lost in the modern Church due to cynicism, skepticism, and sarcasm. It has become so common place that now there is a spirit loosed in Christianity that says you don't have to go to a church building, and you don't need to be a part of a local congregation. Though I completely understand where this is rooted, I could never agree with abandoning visiting with my Father in *His* house. I prefer to rid the house of the things that have defamed it than to abandon it. Yet David was quite resolute that he was married to and settled into the thought that, for the rest of his life, he wanted nothing more than to be found hanging out in the house of the Lord. This kind of commitment and attitude is necessary to fully embrace sanctuary worship. The skepticism has to be done away with, and the loyalty has to return in order for the sanctuary to hold its proper place in the community of believers. Ridding the Church of the skepticism is not easily done in light of the present-day scandals and abuses that are so prevalent. However, if the worshipers will approach the worship setting with the "one thing" mentality that David possessed, they will begin to move themselves into a position where the Lord will protect their desires and direct them to the house of the Lord and steer them clear of houses of worship.

The house of the Lord provides a special and unique environment for the worshipers. It accommodates worship. It contains the furniture necessary for authentic worship, and most importantly, it is only used for worship; nothing else happens in this setting. This is irresistible to the worshiping soul. The coffee house Bible study and the home church, though they can serve a useful purpose, cannot replace the place where YHWH dwells. These other locations have multiple uses. They are designed to facilitate business or commerce or the comfort of a family, so they are not exclusive for worship or the Presence.

But when we look at the type of sanctuary David was in love with, we see that it was a one-of-a-kind setting in which everything about it spoke to the owner's personal preferences. Since David was a worshiper at heart, he was not concerned with some of the things we concern ourselves with today. We look at our churches for their user-friendliness, how well they accommodate our needs, and whether or not they are fun or bright; we concern ourselves with one-stop shopping, if you will, on our church campuses. All of these things are modern phenomenon that have come from our departure from worship as a focus and the redirection to people as the focus.

David's experience in the Presence was so compelling that all of the design, architecture, and setup of his tabernacle and the temple were centered on worship and exposure to the Presence. The fact that our churches have become places of people-accommodation is the reason why people don't come anymore and why we have lost our uniqueness in the community. People change, and if we are seeking to accommodate people, then we must continue to change every time the appetites of the people change. The Church is not McDonalds; we don't have to keep up with or predict the next trend to continue to stay in business. McDonalds is contemporary; the Church is a classic, as is Christ. What we offer and how we offer it is classic and permanently defining for all generations.

Becoming all things to all people does not mean that I am contemporary; it means I am relevant. This works well for me because the Bible is the most relevant, classic, and futuristic book on the planet. It uniquely covers subject matter past, present, and future; and sometimes it even does it all in one verse. So I use a blueprint that allows me to remain truly *classic* while being relevant in my message to the world and at the same time functioning in full preparation for things to come. Why would I want to be contemporary when I'm armed with the Scriptures and the Holy Spirit?

Anyone who comes into and becomes married to the house of the Lord is set in the most distinctive environment in the entire community. Once the worshipers become fully exposed and engaged in this atmosphere, they become addicted to it and will not settle for any other type of corporate worship experience. This setting offers three-dimensional worship (Outer Court, Inner Court, and Most Holy Place), it offers music that goes up like incense before the Lord (not songs designed for people's applause), and it offers instruction and information that equips and prepares the disciple for participation in the kingdom of G-d and entry into the Most Holy Place (not good sermons that *wow* the people). Most importantly, it accommodates the face-to-face worship experience in the Most Holy Place and eliminates the need for personality-driven worship services. This is the experience that the world is awaiting.

So the first facet of this threefold *"one thing"* is *dwelling*. The second facet of it is *beholding*. This word is defined by the Hebrew word *chazah*, meaning "to gaze; to perceive or contemplate (with pleasure), or to have a vision of." These descriptions make it clear that David had entered into a dimension of worship we almost never see in our programmed, structured environments. There is great pause in the worship David experienced. It was not rushed or scheduled to accommodate the next service or a waiting crowd. This type of worship was timeless. Have you noticed how in modern worship we have everything timed so precisely that G-d has limited time to manifest His plan in our worship? We sing three opening songs, move quickly through a brief scriptural exhortation, grab the offering like an assembly line, give you one more song, and then deliver a twenty-three-and-a-half minute message, followed by a very precise and rigid altar call, all in the name of "we have such a large crowd that we have to work within certain parameters." For the larger congregations, everything is done based upon crowd consciousness. In small churches, everything is crowd pleasing, since they don't want to lose the few they have. In all of this, the worshipers have very little time to gaze upon and contemplate the beauty of the Lord.

David must have perceived something so much greater than what we perceive today in our worship services because he sacrificed time just so that he could be contemplative. This is why the video/technology-driven worship services of our day (in all of its contemporary-ness) can never facilitate worship. The images flashing on screens around our sanctuaries are actually designed to be amusing, which is contrary to worship. Since amusement is counterintuitive to contemplation, there is no way we can create a contemplative environment while people are viewing changing camera angles and flashing announcements with background music. These things do not facilitate worship; they facilitate entertainment, which I can get anywhere else in the community.

David was mesmerized with the beauty of the Lord. Now let's keep in mind what he was looking at when considering this Psalm. He was speaking specifically of the Ark of the Covenant. It is the object (the only object that YHWH has authorized) to represent His Presence on the Earth. David had brought the Ark into a tent (tabernacle) that he had designed for it. Now his worship had a focal point that superseded a person or even the tent that it was housed in at the time. David meditated while gazing at it and was filled with joy and security.

This is an experience that the modern Church has never experienced, and one must ask, *Why?* Why is it that we have missed out on this glorious exposure to the shekinah of G-d? The first of many answers is obvious: We have been subliminally disconnected from our Hebraic roots and, therefore, have no real connection to the Ark other than figuratively. Second, we have not designed our sanctuaries to facilitate such a piece of furniture. Our sanctuaries are designed to house the presence of a pastor or a bishop. As a matter of fact, that is what the cathedral was created for. *Cathedral* in its Latin interpretation means "a chair" or, in the religious context, "a bishop's official throne," so the cathedral is the building that houses the bishop's throne. Wow! How many Christians attend a cathedral every Sunday and do not realize that they are worshiping in the place of the bishop's throne. And since we are on the subject, why does a bishop need a throne? Even if thrones were warranted, the bishop is not even one of the five gifts given to the Church by Christ (see Eph. 4:11). Any research on the subject will yield the truth about this false hierarchy that was developed by Catholicism many hundreds of years ago with no scriptural backing or basis. In the past one hundred years, many mainline Protestant denominations have bought into this structure blindly. The designs of our sanctuaries eliminate the opportunity to contemplate the beauty of the Lord.

One more significant difficulty we face today is that our worship services are not patterned after a three-tier framework of progression to move into the Most Holy Place. When I refer back to the Mosaic tabernacle pattern, which represents the origin of corporate worship, there is a threefold pattern that brings us into the fullness of worship. This can be enhanced by the stages of a worship service and the music of that worship service. Again, the Outer Court represents the worship of the sinner—dealing with the flesh. The Inner Court (Holy Place) represents the worship of the saint—dealing with the redeemed soul. And most importantly, the Most Holy Place represents the worship of the Lord—dealing with the spirits of people.

The Psalms of Ascent are of particular value here because they help us to understand that people did not just walk into the Most Holy Place or the Presence of the Lord in general without contemplative preparation. Each Psalm represented a step on the ascent into the temple. As people would rise from step to step, the Psalm would be read and contemplated before they ascended farther. The goal of reading these Psalms in preparation for worship was that, by the time they reached the pinnacle, they had spiritually transcended through the flesh and the soul and had arrived at a spiritual place where they could enter into the fullness of worship.

This is a misnomer to this generation. There is no contemplation in today's worshipers. The modern Christian is completely programmed. When it comes to worship, we go in having already presumed when we will be departing. We go in knowing that on certain Sundays we will do this and on other Sundays we will do that. We walk into a completely worked-out format, which is designed by theologically astute ministry school graduates who understand liturgy styles and origins and are considering the psychological component of what the worship service should supply for the congregant. Essentially, they have programmed the spontaneous and intuitive move of the Holy Spirit right out of the experience.

When Moses transcended from court to court in the tabernacle, it was designed to invoke a spiritual transition as well as preparing him for his entry into the Most Holy Place. No one just walked into the Most Holy Place; they only entered after proper consecration and preparation due to the sin issue. This is why, after Adam sinned, he feared being in the Presence of G-d.

David needed time to take in the glorious beauty (splendor and grace) of the Father's Presence. This cannot be digested quickly, nor does David want to miss what he can gain from this meditation, so he takes his time to fully embrace all that he can in those moments. This is what the Church needs, and this is what the Church is missing. Wherever did we get the notion that two or two-and-a-half hours in worship is enough? How did we manage to reduce the Sabbath to a few hours of worship, and the rest of the day is ours? This trick of the enemy has been effective over the centuries, but is presently being dismantled. Even though we are in the midst of a microwave, short attention span generation, worship will no longer be compromised to satisfy a passing generation. Corporate worship is undergoing an extensive renovation and will emerge in the future as the most vital activity in the Christian's week. It will emerge as powerful and awesome; it will be seen as purposeful and passionate; it will be completely spontaneous, yet completely spiritual.

If the Church is going to see the shekinah in the sanctuary again, it's going to have to completely facilitate it. And this will be the difference going forward between authentic gatherings and those who are insisting on holding on to that which G-d is not using anymore. During our ignorance, G-d allowed us to function at this lower level of worship, but now that a clearer revelation has come, we will have no excuse to continue to use video screens, shopping malls, non-biblical annual traditions, and personality-driven environments to facilitate worship. The bar has been raised, we are unearthing the ancient paths, and regardless of our comfort level, we must walk in them (see Jer. 6:16).

The third part of David's *"one thing"* found in Psalm 27:4 is to *inquire* in His temple. Inquisition is a very necessary part of David's worship experience. The Hebrew word used here is *baqar,* meaning "generally to break forth (as in plowing); and figuratively to inspect, admire, care for or consider, or to search or seek out." So when David entered into worship, there were certain objectives that he was looking to accomplish. It wasn't about just jumping and shouting nor was it about keeping format and following the protocol. David was on a journey every time he entered into this sacred experience.

First, he understood this temple or tabernacle atmosphere provided a unique opportunity for the worshipers to inquire or seek and search out specific information. To take advantage of this was wisdom. There is a component about worship that is designed to supply answers to life's dilemmas, both individual and corporate. There is frustration in contemplation if it is not followed up with inquisition. Contemplation will fuel questions that are wide-ranging, some warranted and some unwarranted. Regardless of the nature of the queries, our Father is gracious, and the Scripture makes it clear that He desires to answer us speedily. But more importantly, there are serious issues surrounding most individual lives that human ministry has been ineffective in answering; these are the ones that G-d wants to take ownership for.

Still we worship with the problem that everything is so programmed that only a few general answers are thrown out during the sermon, and the people still leave the experience with few definitive insights for their lives. What worshipers need is time and a place where they can come and begin to plow through and break up the unplowed territories of their hearts while worshiping. They need time to come to conclusions in the private areas of their hearts where they can be honest with G-d about who they really are and allow the Spirit of G-d to deal with them. This is what the Outer Court and Inner Court pattern of worship should supply for the worshipers. When transitioning through these phases of worship, we have time to come clean before the Lord and open our hearts to His promptings and move into a place where, when the answers come, we can receive them.

When David says that he wants to inquire in His temple, he knows that this is a special place and there is no replacement for it. The temple is like a pavilion, as he goes on to say in the next verse, and he likes to be found hidden in it. This pavilion is reminiscent of an insulated reserve where the enemy cannot find him. This is very different from the coffee shop gathering. This is like an entwined fence used for concealment and protection. I know that our churches have become less than a pavilion, but we have a unique opportunity to return to original intent and redeem the usage of the temple location while the Lord gives us time. In this private and secure location, David could linger and gaze and get answers to life's struggles. Moreover, he could emerge armed with new strategy and execute these strategies to bring him and his nation victory.

Being delivered from the church building and going to church has been a wonderful thing for me and TWC over these past seven years. We have effectively divorced ourselves from dead and meaningless traditions that wasted our time and were rendered irrelevant. We have committed to only practicing things that have scriptural basis and spiritual significance. We have reconnected our theology and practices to our Hebraic roots so as not to drift away on a Gentile notion. But lately we have begun to understand the importance of the sanctuary in our worship. This sanctuary is the "house of the Lord," and not "our church." In this context, we cannot and will not do what *we* think is best in His house. Everything done in His house must be in accordance with His desires and His will and His purposes.

With this type of intense commitment to sanctuary worship, there is a type of enemy insulation that the Lord provides for the worshipers. We see it not only in Psalm 27:5-6, but also in Psalm 91, where this kind of worship yields more than what it yields in today's world. David received spiritual guarantees that angels would be given charge over his life and he would be lifted up high above his enemies. This I believe will also be a catalyst for the demand for authentic corporate worship experiences. People are going to need more and more invisible protection from the unknown that will be attacking humankind going forward.

In days to come, worship will have to be more than just going to a building for a couple of hours. It's going to be a force in the lives of believers. They are going to take command of their lives and their futures while in worship. It will yield the type of insight and information needed so that, while people are in worship, they will cancel a disease or redirect a car accident or keep their children from being victims of a pedophile all while being in the pavilion and inquiring in the temple. When the Church locks on to this kind of power and authority as Heaven's direct response to their worship, we won't be able to keep people out of the sanctuary nor will we be able to limit the time that they are in the Lord's presence.

I believe we can garner this type of attitude from David's worship. He wasn't just meeting a weekly quota or fulfilling some tradition; he was locking into something that was powerful long after he left that sanctuary. He knew that this unique experience gave him victory over his enemies all week long, and his enemies didn't even know why. Wouldn't it be powerful to come out of worship and know what was going to happen in the week to come? This is exactly where the worship is going to take us in the future. Of all of peoples of the Earth, we will be the most envied because of the connection that we have with Heaven.

What happens after this is natural and spontaneous, and I love it. It's called impulsive praise. There is nothing better than to be in a corporate worship environment where the saints just break forth in unprompted praise. On a recent trip to Cote I'voire in West Africa, as I was being introduced to come to the podium and speak, the crowd arose and began to clap and give G-d praise. In a flash, I realized that the sound of the claps could not have been for me. So as I placed my open Bible on the podium, I kept my head down, and I begin to pray and thank G-d. After about a minute or so, I just began to raise my voice in praise to my Father, without interrupting their praise. After about ten minutes, I closed my Bible and realized that there was no way I was going to interrupt this type of praise with my comments or anything I had previously prepared to do. That praise lasted about forty-five minutes, uninterrupted by me or anyone else on a microphone; it was the shekinah that had come in and began to manifest in the midst of the people.

There is something very special about allowing the praise to go unencumbered by our voices and by our input. We see it almost every Sabbath at TWC. We look forward to the moment in worship when we all know it is not about the music, the singers, or the leader; it is all about the Presence. This type of unprompted praise is always a follow-up to worship that yields victorious strategies and information that gives people power over their circumstances. In the future, worship will not in any way be a timed experience. Churches that are attempting to hold on to their synchronized services will soon render themselves irrelevant. The world we live in warrants more time in the sanctuary worshiping corporately. There is no clock displayed in TWC today, and I'm not allowed to wear a wristwatch into the worship. We are constantly reminded by the Holy Spirit that it is the Sabbath Day, not the Sabbath three hours. We don't plan anything on the Sabbath for just that reason. The day is designed for worship, fellowship, and rest. I look forward to my Sabbaths.

There is also another consideration with this type of praise that needs to be acknowledged, and it is demonstrated in David's praise. When David brings the Ark of the Covenant into Jerusalem the second time the proper way, there is a tremendous corporate worship celebration (see 1 Chron. 15:26-29). The celebration is completely centered on the Presence and having the Ark in its proper place among the people of G-d. During this extraordinary worship celebration, David is seen dancing and spinning around in a linen ephod as the Ark is being carried into Jerusalem. David abandoned his royal vestments and his kingly posture to accomplish worship. I often remind people when I use this passage that David was a worshiper before he was a warrior. In this context, David abandoned image and reputation for the purpose of worship.

The first thing we need to digest from this is that David was the worship leader. He instigated this entire experience, and he was not sitting on his high perch watching from a distance as the *peasants* worshiped. How we got to this place where the bishops and pastors and "high" titled leaders simply sit and watch is abominable. We've seen it time and time again. People in a pulpit sit stoic during an exuberant worship experience, acting as if all of that type of worship is beneath them or something. Then when they stand to minister, they are constantly badgering the pew as to why they are responding or shouting while they are preaching. This practice is history. David made it clear that there is no image in worship, but the image of the worshiper. There is no reputation in worship, but to be known as a worshiper. David was not concerned that he was not wearing his kingly garment; neither was he concerned with the fact that the average person was seeing him express himself with this level of humility; he was worshiping!

The imagery that we have brought into worship has, in many cases, ruined worship for those who have wanted to break out into spontaneous praise. We have the very dignified environments, where no one can even say hallelujah without being looked at firmly—to the ones where you can worship, but when we say stop, you have to control yourself—to the ones where everyone can lose it in worship except for the leader in the pulpit who sits deep and reserved during the entire experience, barely exhibiting facial movement. What nonsense! This imagery in no way typifies what is seen in Scripture, especially during Israel's authentic worship experiences. From the days of David and, in many cases, during the Mosaic era, it was a picture of extreme celebration filled with joy and gladness for the goodness of the Lord. David was a worshiper, and whoever despised it paid for it by the judgment of G-d. So it was with Michal in the end (see 2 Sam. 6:20-23).

Once David brought the Ark back into the city of David, he was able to set a new and exciting standard for how corporate worship should be experienced. He departed from the Mosaic practice, though he didn't abandon its pattern, and he implemented an all-day worship practice that demanded the participation of many. David did the unprecedented and was allowed to do so because of his relationship with YHWH and his personal desire for authentic, fulfilling worship.

Sanctuary worship is not going away as some may be predicting. In fact, it has faded to a point of insignificance so that the concept and practice can be reexamined in light of Scripture. I'm grateful for how G-d has allowed the local church gathering to be diminished to the point of *"what's the point?"* Actually, it is providing a platform for it to be resurrected upon an entirely different foundation. As long as there is a temple in Heaven (see Rev. 11:19) and the Ark is in that temple, I have a concrete reason to see what's happening in Heaven manifest in the Earth. The sanctuary of the Lord has been redefined over the years with various designations, from the denominational influences to cultural influences, none of them being satisfactory to its original and eternal framework. Now in this millennium, we have a once-in-a-lifetime opportunity to bring the sanctuary to a place of unique prominence in the community. The future of worship will not be that we abandon what G-d has established as an eternal institution, but rather that we passionately restore it to its spiritual and scriptural significance in the Christian faith.

CHAPTER 9

THE SIGNIFICANCE OF THE TABERNACLE OF DAVID

The main thrust behind *The Future of Worship* is found in the significance of the Davidic tabernacle. What David established had much greater implications than he could have imagined in his day and time. David, by divine providence, introduced a prophetic worship paradigm that would be deemed eternal in nature and most significant for all earthly times.

To comprehend fully what brought David to this prophetic and eternal juncture, we have to journey back through some important stages of his life, namely the time that began with him resting from his enemies. As previously stated, when David was able to rest from his enemies (see 2 Sam. 7), his focus returned to the desire of his heart, which was worship. At the time when David articulated his desire to build a house for the Presence to dwell in, he was also at a stage in life when a man begins to think in terms of his earthly legacy. Yes, he had conquered enemy after enemy, he had exceeded the accomplishments of Saul, and Israel had become unified under his leadership. Yet David was considered by many to be concerned with his legacy and whether or not Israel would forget about him years after his death. So there is speculation as to whether David wanted to build a temple for the Lord that would dually serve as a monument to his earthly accomplishments as leader of Israel as well. This may or may not have been the case, and speculation is duly warranted. Part of this understanding is drawn from the answer that Nathan was given as a response to David's desire.

The Bible says that during that night the word of the Lord came to Nathan to deliver to David. The answer included some clear statements from YHWH that are still pertinent today. YHWH stated clearly that from the time of Moses until David's day, He had never asked anyone to build a house for Him to dwell in. Nor had He asked anyone why they hadn't built a house for Him to dwell in. This is pertinent today because we still see the monuments of our personal glory being built in the name of Jesus year in and year out. What concerns me is that David had a *personal desire* with no *divine instructions*. For him to build based upon a personal aspiration would have been in the end idolatrous. Many of the church buildings, cathedrals, and campuses can be viewed as idols to those who built them. There is nothing wrong with the personal desire; we know that because that is what David started out with. However, once G-d told him he was not to build it, he became content. Does our leadership overlook this fact and forge ahead with their own intent to build according to their own desires as well? When we look closely at the building processes that churches go through, we can conclude that many are driven by personal aspirations.

A few very simple questions can help you understand why I make such a direct critique about church building projects today. Firstly, where did the design come from? There is only one scriptural blueprint for the "house of the Lord." Technically, every worship facility should follow this same pattern and thus minimize the expenditure on architects. Secondly, the sanctuary should be completely paid for before it is erected, as in the case of the Mosaic tabernacle (see Exod. 36:3-7). YHWH would never allow for what He has authorized to be built with funds borrowed from a satanic system of lending and interest compounding. Thirdly, the inspiration to build is never based upon the need to accommodate more people. Since the purpose of the house is exclusively to house the Presence, as long as the Presence is accommodated, there would never be a need to expand for purposes of housing people.

Now I will be the first to admit that all of these reasons seem extreme in the least. However, what we have seen in the evolution of the modern Church is the dramatic expansion of ministry facilities in a competitive way. We see the amazing amount of debt that is incurred (in first world countries in particular) on the backs of the members and future members of those churches. We see how money becomes the driving emphasis with every building project before, during, and after. We see how the churches become cathedrals in deed—buildings that house the throne of that pastor, bishop, or superstar preacher. We see that they become entertainment centers, designed in particular to accommodate this generation's whims and trends. We see that they become monuments of the leaders' personal accomplishments and creativity that will stand for generations to come and will always relate back to them.

YHWH assures David, from Second Samuel 6:8-13, that He had brought him from nothing to this place of greatness among the greatest to walk the Earth, and his seed and throne will be established forever. YHWH's words were designed to let David know that he would be remembered for something far greater than a building. At the same time, David was assured that his desire would be accomplished by his seed and that, more importantly, the throne of his kingdom would abide forever. So G-d would allow a dwelling place to be built because He knew the heart of David and because it facilitated a greater plan down the road, but the glory of that dwelling would not be attributed to David, but to his son. So the physical structure would have a person to whom the connection would be ascribed, yet the eternal connection of *worship* would be credited to David. It's funny how we see Solomon worship, but we do not attribute a heart of worship to Solomon; that forever belongs to David.

All of this is stated so that we can ascribe eternal implications to the life, kingdom, and worship of David. This becomes foundational and should be kept in the context when we look at the tabernacle that David erected for the Ark of the Covenant. David was not allowed to build a temple, but he was allowed to erect a very simple, but significant, tabernacle to house the Presence. It is this tabernacle that is noted in Amos 9:11 as being the only era of worship that would be resurrected and restored to prominence in the future; no other era would be given this distinction. Neither the tabernacle of Moses nor Solomon's temple is earmarked for restoration; neither will the synagogue era, which we understand to be founded upon human ingenuity, ever be given the type of notoriety in worship as the tabernacle of David. This in and of itself should invoke curiosity and research about David's tabernacle and what it implies about corporate worship today.

What stands out the most when contemplating the tabernacle of David is the simplicity of the tent and the exposure of the Ark of the Presence. Again, what David was allowed to do in a time when the Ark had been shielded behind the veil was unprecedented and prophetic. David set in motion a worship paradigm that lasted about forty to sixty years in natural time, but is eternal (as YHWH promised) in its divine context. Here is what we are able to conclude in retrospect about what David initiated thousands of years ago.

First, you have to accept that, according to Amos 9:9-10, only a remnant will be able to receive and embrace the tabernacle of David worship paradigm. Most will debate and reject it because it does not fit into their theological boundaries or because it does not accommodate the focus of modern ministry.

When David erected the tent for the Ark, he transcended the Mosaic setup by bypassing the Outer Court and the Inner Court. This would create a theological problem in his day because it was necessary to go through those other steps in order to get to the Most Holy Place. However, since David's imagery of worship was prophetic, he was looking forward to a time when the focus of worship would be on having a face-to-face experience with the Father, reminiscent of Adam in the Garden in the cool of the day. Adam's experience (before sin) was all about the fellowship, uninhibited and unencumbered. It also looks forward to the time when Christ's death on the cross would put humankind back in that position by virtue of His sacrifice on the cross. Matthew 27:51 makes it clear that, at the point of Jesus' death, the veil in the temple was ripped in two from top to bottom, thereby exposing the Most Holy Place. Just as David foresaw this in his tabernacle worship, Jesus' blood made it completely possible to go into the Most Holy Place and worship the Father face-to-face.

The Hebrews 8 and 9 passages bring this out with great clarity so that there can be even greater significance given to the tabernacle of David. Hebrews 8 sets the tone of tabernacle worship by comparing the earthly copy and shadow to the "true tabernacle," which was not made with earthly hands, but by YHWH Himself. What this means is that Moses was given specific direction to make an earthy tabernacle after the similitude of the one that already existed in Glory, erected by G-d. This is why, when he was instructed to make this tabernacle, he was prohibited from adjusting the pattern even slightly. The pattern he was following was mimicking the true tabernacle, and to adjust it would mean that it was no longer a copy of the original.

What is interesting to me is that this pattern has never and will never be abolished because it represents what exists in Glory. When pastors, bishops, or any spiritual leaders creatively design church facilities and ignore the pattern that has already been designated, they are on their own in building it, and there is no guarantee that Jehovah will come to dwell in that location since the builder did not keep to the pattern and design that was previously ordained. I have concluded some years ago that asking G-d to come by our church and bless us was an indictment on the church. Why would the one for whom the house was built have to be coerced to come and visit it?

When Moses finished building the tabernacle, the Presence descended immediately into that location and stayed there permanently. In the same way, when Solomon finished the temple, the next thing we see is the Presence filling the house like a cloud. The Father is pleased to come and stay when we have designed the sanctuary to be a copy or shadow of what already exists. If there is no similarity, there will be occasional visitation, but no habitation. Habitation only comes because YHWH feels that there is no difference between His dwelling in Heaven and His dwelling on Earth.

So when Christ the high priest of good things to come died, according to Hebrews 9:11-12, He entered into the true tabernacle in Glory armed with His own blood as an eternal sacrifice for sins, and He splashed it before the Father in that Most Holy Place, also referred to as the Holy of Holies. When the Hebrew writer used this term for this divine tabernacle, he used a term that inferred that this is the *holiest* place of all places ever created in all of G-d's creation. Once Jesus entered into this holy location with His blood atonement, there is no need for the barrier to remain in the earthly tabernacle, separating humans from G-d any longer. Thus the veil in the temple was ripped in two, exposing the Most Holy Place, just as David set the Ark of the Presence in a tent exposing the glory of G-d. The image of the rent veil is the image of the Davidic tabernacle.

So the significance is premier in that any modern worship that excludes the exposure and full access of the Presence is in fact insufficient when viewed in light of what Jesus opened the way for on the cross. The blood of Jesus has now brought us back into unique fellowship with the Father. The same fellowship that was lost through the sin of Adam and Eve is now fully restored and should be enjoyed by all who put their trust in that blood.

But look at what the enemy has done. Not only has he obscured the Davidic tabernacle worship paradigm from modern worship, but he has also removed the Most Holy Place from our worship facilities and replaced them with high pulpits and stages with flashing lights. What greater deception could there be to the modern worship experience than to change the entire setup, making it so that the flesh is front and center and receives the glory for what is done in the name of G-d, rather than Jehovah Himself being front and center?

Thousands of years ago, Christianity was hijacked by so-called Roman believers who, instead of conforming to the culture of Christianity and things of Christ, refashioned Christianity to accommodate their cultural perspectives and thus reduced the Abrahamic faith to a religion. It was not long after this takeover that the faith that was, in truth, Jewish became Gentile and assumed the mindset and practices of Gentile-thinking people. This made it easy to redesign the worship facilities with the omission of the Most Holy Place and replacing it with pulpits, podiums, and stages. It made it easy to reorder the responsible offices of the Church (apostle, prophet, evangelist, pastor, and teacher) and replace them with the hierarchy of bishops, pastors, cardinals, deacons, and any array of new titles we have seen lately. It made it easy to change the *focus* of the gathering from pure worship of the Almighty to the delivery of the sermon by the preacher. It made it very easy to replace healing, deliverance, and supernatural manifestation with buying, selling, and celebrating ourselves on a regular basis. The list goes on and on.

Step inside any modern worship facility today, and it doesn't take five minutes to deduce what that ministry is known for. Some of the largest ministries in my city are earmarked by what they are known for. There is one that is known for its amazing choir and singing ability; there is another known for its social and community consciousness; there is another known for the pastor's gift of teaching;

and yet another known for its radical pastor and his preaching. They are filled to capacity on Sundays. Yet YHWH made it very clear to me that the ministry He has given me responsibility over should never be known for any of these things. He told me that if thousands are to gather from week to week, they should gather in that sanctuary for one reason and one reason only—because His Presence has drawn them. The Worship Center will always be known for one thing—the Presence of El Shaddai!

Now for the next five to ten years, I see the future of my worship being built upon the restoration of Davidic worship in the corporate worship setting. G-d says in Amos 9:11 that He will raise up the tabernacle of David, which has fallen down. He will *repair,* meaning "to restore back to its original or healthy state." The corporate worship experience is obviously in an unhealthy state and is in need of several different types of repairs. Since the Father is the only one who can truly comprehend its original state, He will be the one to initiate its restoration. He will *raise it,* meaning "to lift up or make prominent." Only the Father is equipped to make the Church prominent again. If flesh gets involved in the process, we will simply glorify that flesh. So the Father will take it upon Himself to raise the Church up from its ruined and destitute condition.

He will *rebuild,* meaning "it was broken down over time because of neglect and disregard." It's been so long since it has been in its original state of glory that there is no modern leader who has the ancient imagery in his mind to be able to accomplish rebuilding it. Therefore, the Father must step in and rebuild the sanctuary *"as in the days of old"* Himself. The days of old could only be referencing one thing, the brief period of time in which David and the Levites instituted twenty-four-hour worship and all of Israel had access to the Presence of YHWH.

This is where my hope is emboldened and my confidence lies. YHWH Himself will take responsibility for bringing worship back to where it should be. In my mind, this is the tsunami that I've been warning people everywhere is coming to the Church. Those who think that they "run the church" or "are in charge" will be rudely awakened. This will not be something that will be negotiated, voted on, or debated in church meetings, theological institutions, or annual board meetings of denominational leaders. This is something that, when the wave of it hits, there will be no question that G-d has authorized it. I see the shift being dramatic and full of irrefutable evidence.

The contrast between what was considered worship and what will be introduced will be convincing and convicting. People who have yearned and pined for authentic worship will begin to come out of nowhere. The saved and unsaved will begin to flock to the environments that facilitate true worship. Jesus will be lifted in these settings, and He will do the drawing, not the music, not the sermon, not the conference title, not the special event, not the concert, not the celebrity; Jesus Himself will do the drawing, and people will truly be saved and delivered by His Presence. The leaders' job will be to supply the venue, secure the atmosphere, and provide the revelation that brings people closer to the Master. What could be better for the dead, wayward, confused, and disheveled Church than that we have a new opportunity to enter into His Presence with thanksgiving.

This is the resurrection that the Church is seeking. We have tried softening the message, redesigning the sanctuaries, removing religious symbols, dressing down, providing contemporary music, and many other ventures. These measures have only yielded weak and uncommitted church-goers and not powerfully anointed citizens of the kingdom. This move will not come with a new PR team or a new million dollar marketing campaign. It will not come with the *acquisition* of a mortgage disguised as a *celebration* of a new building. False hopes will not be raised because of a new prelate, archbishop, or organizational president who will preside over the same old system of theological tradition. It will come with the authenticity of His presence!

The resurrection of the Church to the power and glory that Jesus promised we would walk in as children of the kingdom will be manifest without superficial human-made accommodations and recommendations. This resurrection will come out of unknown places via uncharted territory. Tsunamis don't ask for permission; they just show up. The Church will experience resurgence in the way that Jesus left those disciples to wait in the upper room. Out of nowhere, those who have been waiting in obscurity will be revealed in power all around the world. It will be organic, not organizational; powerful, not political; supernatural, not superficial. In fact, it will be unprecedented just as David's move to house the Ark in a tent was unprecedented. However, the reason why it was acceptable was because the Lord was truly doing a new thing, and He was letting everyone behold it.

With the introduction of the Most Holy Place to the worship facility, we will finally be able to fully comprehend what the blood of Jesus has done for us. The high priest entered with fear and trembling, having been sanctified externally and internally, hoping that the wrath of G-d would not be unleashed on him because of his sins. We will now have the opportunity to experience just what that priest experienced, having put our trust in the blood of Christ. Hebrews 10:19, which is often referred to as the "hall of faith," will be our starting point since it is faith in the blood of Jesus that gives us the confidence to enter into a *real* Holy of Holies with boldness. This will be a sure way for us to know if we are truly under the blood, walking in trust, and living as redeemed, new creatures in Christ.

For many, this will be viewed as sacrilegious, a denial of the New Testament, strange theology, and so forth. However, since I am not motivated to do any injustice to the blood of Christ, the preeminence of Christ, the indwelling of the Holy Spirit, or any similar accusation that may be raised, I am confident that this revelation about corporate worship will stand against the most interrogating scrutiny. What we are missing today is the Holy of Holies, the Most Holy Place.

What we know is that on the day Jesus died He gave access to that most sacred location, proving it by the ripped veil. What we are sure of is that the Romans gave the Church its present worship facility design. What we cannot find in Scripture is where G-d deemed the Mosaic pattern for His house obsolete and where the adoption of a new pattern or design was introduced or G-d decided to leave it up to us to design a new pattern for His house. What we can stand on scripturally is that David's prophetic tabernacle (worship paradigm) is the only tabernacle that the Father says He will re-raise in this day. It is also conclusive that the tabernacle is of greatest significance because it will welcome the Jew and Gentile in worship at the same time. We also must agree that James sights this Scripture in his discourse in Acts 15 to open the New Testament Church up to the revelation of David's prophetic tabernacle design and pattern of corporate worship so that it would not be written off as an Old Testament concept.

What must happen now is that the Church must become humble and submissive to the Head of the Church. We must admit that, in all of our technological, intellectual, financial, and strategic maneuvers, we have come up short in our ability to exhibit the power that those Holy Ghost-filled disciples exhibited. We have also not fulfilled our kingdom mandate in the earth by birthing and revealing the children of G-d. We must acknowledge that we have not walked in the dominion that Christ reinstated for us when He was resurrected on that great day. I believe these things are in direct relation to the Church's disconnect in worship. If Christ were to release us into the power, dominion, and revelation that we should be walking in under these incorrect circumstances, we would never be moved to seek corrections to our practices.

Right now, the Church is searching for answers globally. The denominational structure is losing validity daily. People are disenchanted by religious systems and will not continue to worship ignorantly and insincerely. Though the world is lost in its futility, there is and will always be the void that the love of G-d is waiting to fill, and this desire will be filled in the right corporate worship setting. That setting will have David's fingerprints all over it. It will look and feel like nothing we have ever experienced before, and it will go against all previous tradition without being rebellious. It will be unprecedented, which means there will be no proper judgment to stand against it because it carves out new and uncharted territory. However, one thing will be certain. If the Lord is raising up, repairing, and rebuilding this tabernacle worship, then there will be nothing that any human can do to stop it.

One significant acknowledgment and alteration will revolutionize the Church forever. Presently, the Church's future is quite predictable if we continue on the path that we presently tread. We can predict that, based upon the generation that is presently being groomed to take positions of importance in the world over the next twenty years, the Church will not be a part of their weekly, monthly, and in many cases, yearly routine. We can predict that large denominations will continue to sell their properties to non-denominational groups that are more vibrant and relevant. We can predict that scandal and immorality will continue to plague every religious group that does not embrace the empowerment of the Holy Spirit. We can predict that the modern Church will continue to produce nominal, impotent, dependent Christians who lack maturity. And the list can go on and on.

Yet one major change can and will rewrite the future of the Church, and it is worship. It will bring even the most wayward into relationship with the Lord. It will make the corporate worship gathering irresistible again. It will enable Christianity to liberate itself from its divisions and find new and valuable unity around the Presence of YHWH. It will bring morality and holiness back to the Body of Christ the way Christ intended when He departed. It will produce powerful, Spirit-filled, and kingdom-minded saints who are determined to fulfill their purpose before their departure. It will produce a group of people who will be known for the gifts of the Spirit and not for their hierarchal titles and positions.

The Church has a bright and glorious future, and its worship will be seen as the most valuable thing in the world. Gatherings will be characterized by the Presence of YHWH, just like in the days of David and Moses. Every other nation knew that Israel had something that they lacked and desired to some degree. I see worship in this same way in the future; the Church will be known for possessing a Presence that can't be found or duplicated anywhere else in the world. If this is not the case, I know that I would give up on worship and try to find value in something else this life has to offer. However, my trust is that there is nothing greater in my future than to know that I can go to Father's house and find Him there waiting for me each time I enter those gates.

I end this chapter with four things that we have to look forward to in the future of worship. The first is that there will be a new reverence for the Presence. Just as in the days of Saul, today the Presence has been taken for granted by the Church. There was a time, even in my lifetime, when the Presence was revered and honored, but now we are more awestruck by the celebrity ministers than we are by the presence of G-d. When you track the Ark from the days of Joshua till the time of David, you will find that after Israel came into the Promised Land, they gave less emphasis to the Ark. I believe that is similarly the case today. The more prosperity and notoriety the Church enjoys, the less the Presence is accentuated in the corporate setting. However, in the future it will be the only thing that the worshiper clings to. Nothing else will receive the honor or significance that the shekinah will receive.

Along with this glorious manifestation of G-d's Presence will come the honor and gratitude that is due to His name. This honor and gratitude will be defined by the sacrifices that we bring to the worship experience. No longer will the congregation have to be coerced or manipulated into giving; rather the worshiper will *bring* a sacrifice as a sign of respect, gratitude, and honor toward the Lord. The motivation for giving will be directly related to the Presence that is before them and not the ability of someone to coerce them into giving. The cheerful giver scenario will truly be seen when the environment and atmosphere are properly aligned and focused.

Second, as with David's tabernacle, we must re-define who is responsible for the shekinah. David made sure that he appointed those who should be responsible for maintaining the proper atmosphere and environment for the Presence to dwell. The sons of Asaph were given this responsibility to execute it every day, all day and all night. Some were to praise, some were to play their instruments, some were to guard and stand watch, but every one of them had a responsibility to secure the glory in the midst of Israel. We have not done this well in the modern Church. In most churches, the responsibility has fallen on one or two people, namely the pastor or a musical leader. What needs to be done is that we reinvestigate David's assignments and motivations behind the assignments so that we can get the proper understanding of *who* should be doing *what*.

Third, there must be a revival of the celebration of the shekinah. Once the shekinah was returned to the midst of Israel, David went about creating a sound and songs that would be pleasing to the Lord and not to him personally. Most of our music is designed to please the human listener and not the heavenly listener. David celebrated the shekinah by creating a sound of music different from what we hear today. We must not forget that the music that is conducive to the Father does not cater to our personal preferences. It must cater to the one whose Presence we are going to enter into at that moment, just like the incense before the entrance to the Most Holy Place. David wanted to make sure that the sound was acceptable to the Father. The worldly beats and chords and changes have to be done away with. They may sound good to us because that's what we are used to hearing in the street or on the radio, or it may accommodate our cultural upbringing, but that does not interest our Father. The celebration of the shekinah is the celebration of a sound that He will be pleased with; there must be no more strange fire in holy worship.

Fourth and most importantly, we must provide access to the shekinah. In the future of worship, there will be a clear distinction between synagogue-style churches and temple-style churches. The distinction will be simple—the Holy of Holies. We cannot provide access to the Most Holy Place if it doesn't exist. Just as I am attempting to establish at TWC, thousands of churches will do also; they will create a Most Holy Place. For some, the idea does not fit their theology, and for others, it is Old Testament and represents something that we legitimately left behind when Christ came.

Yet whatever argument you may level against this paradigm shift, one thing is for sure; having a Most Holy Place provides an earthly location where the Father can dwell (between the cherubim) in the house we call His. Yes, we are the temple of the Holy Spirit, and I will never refute what is obvious, but corporately we cannot worship what is inside of us. When we come together corporately, we worship who is before us, and the Church must move away from worshiping the preacher, prophet, bishop, pastor, and so forth who stand before us each day while saying we are worshiping the Father. We are safe in giving people access to the place where Jesus came to remove the barrier from. If that barrier is truly removed and we truly have access to the Father through the Son, then the Church needs an opportunity to prove that out with a tangible location. The Church needs a Most Holy Place!

We took chances in our most recent history by removing the traditional podium and pulpit and replacing it with simple stages. We have removed the choir stand for risers. We have removed the altar and replaced it with beautiful flowers and plants. We removed the large cross and put up revolving globes. We have removed the pews and replaced them with comfortable theatre seating. We have removed the vestibule and replaced it with lounges, cafes, bookstores, and game rooms. So why not eradicate all of that unbiblical stuff and replace it with what we know is in the Scriptures? If anything, we already know that all of this buying and selling is a turnoff to Jesus anyway. Let's see if we can turn Him on by resetting His house in the way that He originally and permanently desired and designed it. Let's give the Church back the Holy of Holies!

Upon returning to this biblical precedent, we can provide instruction to the Church on how to enter into this most sacred place. We can provide revelatory teaching and preaching that empowers the saints with an understanding that they can have access to the Father by the blood of Christ and not by some human standard. We can spend our time dwelling, beholding, and inquiring in His tabernacle. We can see the broken, bruised, and abused go in one way and come out another way. We can see the healing and deliverance we have talked about come to pass before our eyes. What could be better for a Church that has lost its prominence and distinction in the world today? What could be better for a group that has tried everything under the sun to regain its significance in the world and come up empty? What could be better than to go back to the ancient paths and find the good way and walk in it?

My prayer is that the future of worship would be imagined from its history. It is my hope that we will go back to go forward, that we will become humble that we might be exalted. If we use the lens of our historical vantage point, we will see that if we continue the way that we are going, our demise is imminent. If we can see the significance of the tabernacle of David in our day and time and properly use its prophetic insight as foresight, we can forecast how the sanctuary will be restored to a place where the lost can be saved and Israel can be restored.

CHAPTER 10

THE WHO, WHAT, WHEN, WHERE, AND HOW OF WORSHIP

One of the problems with contemporary Christianity is that it doesn't ask the right questions about worship. We have of late adopted such a corporate business attitude about the business of the Church that we are only asking questions as it relates to business and not worship. In a recent conference of pastors that I attended, there was a brief commercial about an upcoming leadership gathering that would feature some of the most well-known voices in the secular marketplace who would be lending their expertise in this setting. It was advertised that never before had a church's leadership entertained such a wide array of experts who were making themselves available in a religious gathering. We would be privy to the secrets and successful business strategies of multi-nation and multi-billion dollar corporations. In further advertising what we would be getting in this conference, the announcer stated that we would be given strategies for how to better understand our clients and how to identify and capitalize on our demographic.

Wow! I said to myself, *This is amazing!* We are now going to get our cues and strategies from the world because they have obtained, in their sphere, notable success. Essentially, they were saying that the world has better and more effective strategies for customer service and client satisfaction (in their business terms) and that the Church needs to look to the world in order to learn how to better serve their client base. Interesting!

I am very much aware that many large denominations and church networks have taken on this paradigm for doing ministry and that many contemporary churches now look at their worshipers as clients whom they are attempting to better serve so that they can continue to get their repeat business. Our "brilliance" will now contribute to our further breakdown. To some degree, we should know better since the last well-known paradigm shift that swept through many of our contemporary churches was assessed (admittedly by the leader) as an incredible expenditure of funds and human hours that produced less than stellar substance in their client base. We must learn from this lesson.

There is a classic New Testament story that gives tremendous insight into what most churches are attempting to accomplish via secular marketplace strategies. It is found in John 4, and it is the story of Jesus and the woman at the well in Samaria. This classic conversation between Jesus and a seeker gives us just about everything we need in order to answer the questions set forth in this chapter.

If we pick up the story where Jesus initiated the dialogue with the woman, we must first acknowledge that Jesus created intrigue in the mind of the potential seeking worshiper. This is one thing that the Church has completely lost the art for. While we are going about defining our demographics and surveying our neighborhoods, we fail to create real intrigue. The intrigue that Jesus created in His initial comment had nothing to do with religion and everything to do with what she was already doing. We are aware that even the fact that Jesus spoke to the woman is striking since there was a historical skirmish between Jews and Samaritans. Yet in His speaking to her, He simply met her at the level she was currently functioning at, thus creating intrigue and not suspicion. Once she responded, He began to speak to her from a spiritual plateau, while she responded to Him from a carnal plateau.

Her response about her cultural background versus His was the basis of her response; however, it was posed as a question warranting an explanation of sorts. The problem today with the approach of Christians to non-Christians is that, in most cases, the Christian is trying to *make* a believer out of someone who is not asking *how* to become a believer. I am always struck by how the jailer in Acts 16 says to Paul and Silas, *"What must I do to be saved?"* rather than Paul or Silas saying, "We think you need to get saved!" If what the Church has is so invaluable and precious to the life of a human, why isn't every human asking for it? The primary reason is that the world doesn't see our worship as invaluable to life, and therefore, they write off Christianity as just another empty, powerless religion. What I would love to see is people who are so intrigued by the life and power of the Christian life that they begin to ask, "How can I get what you have?"

Jesus responded to the woman from His spiritual plateau, attempting to move her from her carnality by stating, *"If you knew the gift of God, and who it is who says to you, 'Give Me a drink,' you would have asked Him, and He would have given you living water"* (John 4:10). Jesus' spiritual statement about living water was designed to steer her clear of religion and generate spiritual intrigue. We cannot seduce ourselves into thinking that providing everything our clients desire is going to, in the end, produce spiritually-empowered people. We have done such a great job of making sure that the people who attend our churches are happy and satisfied with their experience that we've forgotten that we are supposed to be providing an environment that challenges and arrests their dead spiritual state.

In her next response, the woman stayed true to her carnal mindset by stating that Jesus had nothing to draw water with and, therefore, she didn't see how He would be able to provide that living water He was talking about. She further elaborated from a traditional context, which in turn elucidated her religious perspective by including Jacob in her response. Mentioning Jacob as a Samaritan, while talking to a Jew, would definitely provoke some type of religious argument. However, Jesus' response was not argumentative, but enlightening and all the more intriguing. Jesus' response about the water from Jacob's well rang true with her because she was well aware that it did not extinguish thirst.

This must have really gotten her attention because, at that point, she abandoned her loyalty to Jacob's well and requested the water that He was offering. What is amazing about what Jesus had just accomplished is that, other than sticking to the issue of water, He did not have to compromise or accommodate her contemporary views. Instead, she moved away from what she believed and shifted her trust toward His perspective of satisfying water. What this says is that Christians do not have to abandon their positions or belief systems to make the gospel more palatable for the unbeliever. Yet this seems to be the new approach to sharing the gospel and the new paradigm of corporate worship. Almost every pastor or minister I talk to about this subject confirms their submission to the way of the unbeliever, while thinking that they have actually moved to a more relevant form of worship. I hear of the "Friday Night Live," the "R.A.G.E," the "Unplugged," the "Youth Unleashed," and many other hiply-titled type services that are supposed to be the epitome of relevancy, while in fact they are just submitting to the contemporary pressure that this generation has put on anything that is classic.

I often wonder what it will be like when this generation becomes the leadership of these churches in the next ten or so years. By the time they assume the leadership roles, every service will be a concert or stage show, with smoke and flashing lights, because that's what they're being raised on. They won't know how to worship without all of the special effects and technology antics. And the truth be told, many churches would lose a large portion of their congregations if they took away all of their special effects in worship. We must stop satisfying the carnal appetites of people while camouflaging it as being more relevant.

Jesus didn't stoop to the woman's carnal level of thinking; He stayed true to His premise and maintained that what He had to offer her was better than what she was looking for. As a result, she let go of her belief system and agreed to try His. Once this happened, once she submitted to what Jesus was saying, He could move aggressively to bring her out of sin and into salvation.

Jesus, by the Spirit, asked her to bring her husband to be a part of this special moment in her life, and she answered honestly that she had none. Again, because Jesus was functioning in the Spirit and feeding off of divine information, He received a word of knowledge about her past and shared it with her. Once this happened, she no longer viewed Him as just another Jew; she called Him a prophet. This is the commentary that is too often missing from our interactions with the unbeliever. Anytime unbelievers come in contact with saints who are walking in the dimension of the Spirit, they should conclude that they are functioning at a much lower level of existence. Once Jesus answered her the way that He did, with this information, she realized that this guy was functioning at an entirely different level than she was.

Unbelievers don't need their lifestyles and views to be confirmed by the Church's actions; they need to realize that, because the Church functions so differently, the Church has something they need. This woman concluded that Jesus had information about life that she didn't have, and she was going to tap into it at that very moment to satisfy a longing of her heart.

She moved quickly to inquire of this prophet about an issue that she had probably had on her heart for years. The issue is authentic worship. This is, in fact, the bottom line of every religious group and every spiritual experience—authentic worship. Every religion claims not only to be worshiping the correct "god," but to also know the correct way to worship that god. This is the issue that the Church needs to address presently.

In her statement, she immediately stated her position and the opposing positions concerning authentic worship. At the same time that she mentioned it, by default, she was alluding to her confusion and her quest to know how to make a connection with G-d. This is what the Church must shift attention to and capitalize on today. We are so busy trying to fill our churches with people who are happy and satisfied on *their* terms that we have forgotten the terms that the Father has already established (long before this generation existed) about what is acceptable worship for Him. So let's take a good look at what she asked and how Jesus responded to her queries.

Her statement included at least four preconceived notions about worship from her perspective and the Jewish perspective (see John 4:20). The four notions are tradition, location, culture, and religion. These four perspectives represent the basis for her understanding about worship. We need to look at all of them to understand the who, what, when, where, and how of worship today.

Her first stumbling block to authentic worship was her tradition. She said, *"Our fathers,"* meaning this was what was passed down to her over the years. She didn't realize it, but what was passed down over the years was the reason why she was suffering from inauthentic worship at that moment. Her worship understanding was passed down to her over hundreds if not thousands of years without any type of re-examination. No one was checking through history for human error or erroneous opinions that were injected over personal disputes or interpretations. Instead, they just passed it down from generation to generation without any investigation. Most Christians have no historical knowledge of the evolution of the Church at all.

The Church today blindly follows what has been done as if to question it, challenge it, or change it is a cardinal sin.

In 2004, I attended a conference for pastors and ministry leaders in New Jersey. I could have left after the first day. It was on that very first day that a speaker made mention of the Church's ignorance of its history. The statement hit me between the eyes, and the Holy Spirit made it clear that the statement was for me. As soon as I got home, I began to do some serious research on the history of the Christian Church. Throughout my years in Bible school and in some other forms of formal and informal biblical education, I had only barely been made aware of our history. I found three very good reference books on the subject and began to educate myself about the history of the organization that I had been a part of since I was eight years old.

It was the best thing I could have ever done. As a result, I took TWC through an extensive Bible study on this subject with textbook and all. It revolutionized the way we approached Christianity, worship, and the traditions we once held to so dearly. Once we came through that study, we not only understood where and how some things came about, but we understood how valuable it is to go back to Scripture and abandon vain, human-made traditions at all cost. Many of these traditions held us hostage and kept us from experiencing an authentic worship experience. We also noticed how and why so many people had left the Church (though they still embrace Christ as Savior) and feared ever coming back. The traditions in many cases were the very thing that had hurt or hindered their faith and theological understanding.

This poor woman wanted to worship, but was bound up by the traditions of her forefathers. If she was going to understand what worship was supposed to be about, she was going to have to release herself from those traditions that make the Word of G-d ineffective. Jesus spoke about this to the Pharisees in Matthew 15:3 as they attempted to challenge him about breaking tradition. Whenever we go against age-old traditions, we are going to be in for a fight. I can remember when the Christ Gospel Baptist Church transitioned to what is now known as The Worship Center; there were casualties of that war. I will never forget watching the congregation shrink down to twenty-five members, and even then, all of those weren't in agreement with what G-d was doing. Killing sacred cows may seem to cost you everything as you go through it; however, when the dust clears, you will see the will and purposes of G-d clearly exposed. I thank G-d for great grace during those difficult years.

Take some time and re-examine the traditions you hold to. Find out what their origins are and under what circumstances these things were established. Go through the history of your church organization or denomination and compare the practices to the Scripture, and you will get a clear picture as to whether or not your worship is being hindered by tradition or released by scriptural compliance. Embracing scriptural mandates over human tradition has taken the worship at TWC to a whole new level. We see the favor of G-d continually as we give Him what He asks for and not what we think we should give Him.

What we must own up to is that *"our fathers"* could have been sincerely wrong, or they could have been doing the best they could with the dimension of revelation that was available at that time. As we discover more about the Father and His desires, we are able to serve Him and worship Him more appropriately. Just because we have been doing something for one thousand years does not mean that it is right. Furthermore, even if it was right at some point, it may not be what the Father is doing today. Remember that in the transition from Mount Gibeon to Mount Zion, it was not that something was wrong with the Mosaic tabernacle, but that YHWH was not using that context any longer. That's what made Solomon's transition so difficult at first. What do we do when G-d has moved on? My suggestion is to move on with G-d. Moses and the children of Israel had to learn this in their wilderness travels; when the cloud moves, we move. Sometimes it remained for a day or as much as a year, but when YHWH moved on, it was time to pack it up and move with the cloud.

The second thing that the woman was struggling with in her worship was location. She said, *"Our fathers worshiped in **this mountain**."* Now we discover that she was struggling with worshiping in the right location. She had been taught that location rendered your worship authentic or inauthentic. She felt like, if she could get the location right, it would solve her worship dilemma. To this day, the Church still suffers from an improper understanding of this issue.

Chances are that, as a Samaritan, she was following in the footsteps of the Pentateuch primarily from Abraham to Moses, which led them to Mount Gerazim at Shechem. This being the case, we can trace her location issues beginning with Genesis 12:6-7, where Abraham was moving through Canaan to the place of Shechem. This is also the location where Jacob purchased and erected an altar and worshiped (see Gen. 33:18-20). In Deuteronomy 11:29, Moses was told to bless Mount Gerazim and curse Mount Ebal. This scriptural acknowledgment of a location was sure to keep the Samaritans in allegiance or bondage to that particular location. There is further recognition of Mount Gerazim as a place of blessing in Deuteronomy 27:12, which helps to create the struggle in her theology. Still, the greatest argument would come from Joshua 8:33, where the Bible says that even the strangers who were born among Israel would be included in the worship on Mount Gerazim. As a result, this creates a strong and compelling argument in her estimation for struggling with this location versus that location.

Over the years, this issue has been dealt with in various ways based on a variety of opinions and interpretations. I am obviously an advocate of sanctuary worship. The practice of going to the sanctuary on the Sabbath day is scriptural and a necessary part of the Christian lifestyle. We should not forsake the assembling of the saints, which has become the habit of many. Yet at the same time, I believe that worship is not limited to the sanctuary location, especially in this era we call the dispensation of the Holy Spirit. Since the Holy Spirit dwells within the saints, we have the opportunity to worship anywhere without restriction. It should be common for Christians to worship at home or in the car on the way to work. These times of worship are obviously not a part of the corporate worship experience, but rather the individual worship experience.

The problem comes in when people are made to believe that they cannot worship in any other place than the church building. This restriction is religious and constricting. If worship was in fact limited to and authenticated by a location, it would eventually do exactly the thing that happened to Israel during its tabernacle and temple days. Since Israel knew that they had the location and times right, they eventually removed their hearts from the experience. G-d in His wisdom knew from the beginning that having a location would sooner or later produce callous and heartless worship. The location would be taken for granted, just like we see today, and people would simply view it as a place to come when they needed something from G-d or wanted to fulfill a religious quota.

When the woman at the well raised this issue, she was probably thinking, *If I can get the location right, then I can fulfill my religious responsibility with ease.* Yet at the same time, she did not realize that, though she may be fulfilling a religious duty, her spiritual involvement may still be deficient. In large part, many people still view their religious activity in this light. Going to a building, doing something religious, having their name on a membership log, or celebrating a religious holiday is somehow all they need to do to be in right standing with G-d; it is not so.

The other problem is that the teaching that the woman had received had led her to believe that worship is about a location, and this erroneous teaching was keeping her from participating in fulfilling worship. How many people go to a church building when their lives are out of control, thinking that being in that location is somehow going to cause G-d to be moved to bring about a resolution in their lives? How many people avoid a church building because they think that going to that location is somehow going to be viewed as hypocritical or insincere? Either way, the location has kept people from experiencing a truly satisfying worship experience.

If only this woman had known that she could worship anywhere at any time. If only she had known that no one had a a religious advantage on a location that G-d was more partial to than another. If only she had begun worshiping in her home or during her walk to the well or any place that she had time to reflect on the Lord, she would have been so much better off. If only she had realized that the "where" does not override the "who" of worship. I believe that she was so distracted by the proper location that she was ignorant to the fact that she could be in the right location and still not know who she was worshiping. This in turn would still render her worship frustrating and unsatisfying because she was missing the main point of worship.

This issue of *where* separates families and churches to this day. The root of the issue may be more racial than it is local. Jesus addressed this in His response, which we will see shortly. The decision of where to worship is often subtly influenced by who is already worshiping in that location and whether or not we can assimilate with them. The location is the very thing that separates us to this day. If only this division were abolished, we might see a more powerful and united Church.

Third, in this same statement she says, *"And you Jews,"* thus giving insight to the cultural divide that existed between the Jews and Samaritans. So her next difficulty was, "Which culture has it right?" Do the Jews have the right cultural formula, or do the Samaritans have the right formula?

To this day in America, we can still find the morning hours on any given Sunday the most culturally-segregated time of the week. Blacks have their style of worship, while whites have their style.

Asians worship a little differently from Latinos, and the list can go on and on. How did we get to the place where the culture or race of a people came to dominate the context of a Christian group? I'm offended when I hear the term *black church*. I often ask people if they are going to a black Heaven. Paul said it masterfully in First Corinthians 1, but it seems as if the Church has never reconciled his words to our present state—*"Is Christ divided?..."* (1 Cor. 1:13).

The enemy has been masterful in strategically making culture preeminent in the minds of Christians rather than the kingdom of G-d. If the truth be told, that may just be the crux of the problem in Christianity. For over 1,800 years, we have been duped into viewing Christianity as a religion and not a culture. If Christianity were a religion and Rome viewed it as such, then it is a component of the culture. However, that thinking is contrary to the comprehensive nature of Christianity. Since Christianity covers every aspect of the culture (language, family, education, finance, politics, and religion), it is a culture in and of itself. Therefore, the culture of Christianity should override the culture of the individual, who is now a member of the Body of Christ.

At TWC, we had a mantra many years ago that we still adhere to today. It is, *"I am the church, I am a member of the Body of Christ, and I am a citizen of the kingdom of G-d."* What this did for us was make our citizenship in the kingdom the premier thing in our lives. Once I have taken this to heart, I am able to fellowship with anyone of any earthly culture who is a Christian because being a part of the Body of Christ supersedes every other category of culture or race.

Yet today, especially in America (and there are many who perpetuate this), people are almost adamant about fellowshipping with "their own" exclusively in the Church. This in turn assists in keeping worship a cultural thing rather than a kingdom thing. Still, in the long run, in this distorted American culture, we don't even give people the benefit of being a part of a culture. We reduce people to a race based upon their skin color, which deepens the divide. People of a certain color are categorized by their hue even before they are able to introduce themselves and their culture. As a result, we have a large majority of Christianity that worships based upon a racial assimilation rather than a cultural assimilation, and in both cases, they miss out on the wonderful experience of worshiping with others based upon the superseding cultural assimilation of the kingdom of G-d.

Christ did not come and die for us to remain divided upon the simplistic variations of human peculiarity. In fact, before Jesus moved deep into His ministry, John announced that, *"He came to His own, and His own did not receive Him. But as many as received Him, to them He gave the right to become children of God..."* (John 1:11-12). Jesus had in mind the unifying of divided human nature as a part of His ministry from the beginning. We have in fact ruined one of Christ's deepest values in the kingdom (unity) through this divisive issue of race and culture.

I view this poor woman in light of so many people who would be worshiping in a local congregation today, but are discouraged because of the stumbling block of culture and race. They are hungry for truth just as she was, they have a desire for worship just like she did, and they are equally confused about the entire process because of what they have been told about the environment and the experience. Worship is not about natural culture; it never has been and never will be. Worship is about the culture of the kingdom, and anyone who is a part of the kingdom must advocate that culture above every other culture. Once this becomes a part of the DNA of the Church, we will see people of other colors, races, and cultures like the Father sees them—as diverse worshipers in the same family. If the Heaven we are going to will be of the extraordinary diversity spoken of so clearly in Revelation 7:9, why must our experience on Earth be so different? The Father made us with this diversity for His own pleasure, and we have perverted it with the help of a very deceptive enemy to be a concrete reason why we are not able to worship together.

The truth is that there is a tsunami coming, and I've heeded the warning over ten years ago. The technology advancements of our time have started joining people together of diverse cultural backgrounds and races all over the world who have no prejudice about who they connect with. As a result, the wave of multi-cultural anything and everything has long since hit the globe in a way that may not be notable for another ten years. However, what is already happening is that there is a generation developing that has no regard for boundaries the way previous generations did. It's almost like, because of the advancement of global communications, there is *"no sea"* that divides us anymore (see Rev. 21:1).

The shrinking of the world and the advancement of visual and virtual communicative systems allows people to see and speak to people whom they only heard stories about previously. Now those stories, many of which were inaccurate, can be repudiated by people representing themselves face-to-face. Those who are holding on to the old systems of thinking and functioning will be hit with a wave so hard that it may cause death. If there is anything that technology has done for sure, it has brought people of diverse backgrounds, races, and cultures together for personal dialogue and interaction like no other generation has known.

There is a worship experience that is ready to embrace this reality, and it's not the one where Jews don't interact with Samaritans. Once the culture of the kingdom is fully adopted into our worship experiences, we will see worshipers flood into the local congregations like never before. I know this Samaritan woman was confused about it when she began this conversation with the Master, but as we know, when she leaves, it will no longer be her stumbling block.

Last, the conclusion of her question stated, *"Jerusalem is the place where one ought to worship."* When she added this to the context of her query, she exposed the controversy in her mind of religion superseding. Jerusalem represented the powerful epicenter of all religious activity. Even to this day, Jerusalem is seen as the religious headquarters of the world. So she raised the issue of Jerusalem, thus raising the issue of religion as it relates to authentic worship. If religion (Jerusalem) played a major role in the practice of worship, then she would forever be excluded from enjoying what the Jews enjoyed in worship since she was a Samaritan.

Clearly, religion has done just that over the years. So many people I talk to who no longer attend a church setting use this argument all the time. The main reason for their abstinence is that they refuse to be a part of organized religion. They say emphatically that it is controlling and polarizing. It makes them feel continually like they are not good enough. It imposes rules and regulations upon them that they don't even believe the leadership is following. It was true in Jesus' day, and it is still true now.

The truth is that religion actually keeps people from worshiping the Father. Jesus ranted on the scribes, Pharisees, and lawyers for their religious stronghold on the people in Luke 11:37-52. A close examination of these verses reveals that the motivation for Christ's statement was the religious framework of that day and how it hindered those who were attempting to connect to the Father through religion (see Luke 11:52). They had worked hard to set up boundaries that looked moral and spiritual on the outside, but lacked the substance that brought men and women closer to G-d. This practice eventually caused spiritual death to those who practiced such foolishness. Religion was originally crafted by people to give the worshiper the key of knowledge for how to connect effectively back to the Father. However, in the long run, all it has done is take away the key of knowledge, and neither the teacher nor the follower has entered into a more vital relationship with their G-d.

This is the main reason why religions of every sort will eventually fail. They are driven by human ingenuity and deduction. They lack true revelation and leave no space for the sovereignty of G-d to override their contrived processes. People of the twenty-first century who have been reared in a godless society will have no tolerance for the foolery that has existed for hundreds if not thousands of years. The twentieth-century generation that tolerates or makes excuses for a pedophile priest, a false and imposing hierarchy, a scripturally ignorant preacher, a visionless church, a prophet whose words hit or miss, a powerless spiritual leader, or a homosexual worship leader is fading fast. There is a remnant from this group, however, that is not willing to go to a worship environment that openly compromises the things written in the Scriptures. They will avoid these settings completely rather than subject themselves to a false religious system. It is this remnant that will aggressively seek to remove the religious façade from our worship experiences and replace them with authentic environments that assist people in making the connection to YHWH. This will be the saving grace for the twenty-first century generation that knows nothing about church because their parents avoided organized religion entirely during their upbringing.

We live in a religious environment that almost mimics the time in which Jesus walked the Earth to a tee. It is full of religious rivalries and opposing doctrines. It is divisive to the point where the people are only incidental. It has forgotten its mission and purpose for existence. It is in need of a radical realignment, but those who are attempting to do it are clueless. People are going to church, but there is very little heart transformation. We really need the Head of the Church to make an appearance right about now. It would do us all some good.

Since Jesus spent almost His entire ministry undoing religion (and the Gospels attest to this), we should understand that religion is the hindrance. This poor woman probably had it in her mind that she would never be able to worship sufficiently if she had to go through Jerusalem, so why bother? She was probably at a loss and figured maybe this Jewish prophet could ease her worship dilemma by giving her an alternative. This is largely the way people function today. This is what made television pastors so popular, and now streaming church is the alternative for the twenty-first century Christian.

What they are really saying is that they don't want the religion that they are subjected to by going to the building, so they will just watch it on television or, better yet, experience it live by streaming online. At the same time, the religious system is fine with that because now they can collect people's money via credit card and not have to deal with the wayward husbands, drug-abusing children, or any other problems that people may have. It works out just fine for the cost.

Since when is a television broadcast or Internet stream an alternative for being in the Presence? The contemporary Church has lied to itself to justify these practices largely because they serve the purpose of making them feel like they are reaching more people through these mediums. However, what they fail to realize is that people don't go to church because they don't want religion, and that's all they are offering. If they knew that the environment offered a tangible relationship with the Father through His Son, they would never settle for sitting at home watching a screen. They would come sick, depressed, inappropriately dressed, high, drunk—it wouldn't matter; the driving motivation would be, "If I can get in His presence, everything will be made right!"

Worship has nothing to do with religion because when Adam met his Father *in the cool of the day,* all he had was a relationship. All Adam had to do was show up and converse; there was no fanfare, no stipulations, no protocol, but just fellowship, which is the essence of worship. If we can recapture this concept and put it in the framework of the Scriptures, we might be on our way back to a worshipful environment. The wonderful thing is that YHWH still desires this from His creation. He hasn't changed. We have added a ton of unnecessary ingredients into the mixture, but He remains consistent in that He is still seeking true worshipers.

So these four elements represent the woman's dilemma in worshiping effectively. Her query made it clear that she not only wanted to worship, but wanted to worship authentically, and she was hoping that this prophet would give her some insight as to how to accomplish her goal. So now we must unpack Jesus' answer to see how He resolved her difficulty and caused her to become a true worshiper.

Jesus started out by imploring faith of the woman when He said, *"Believe me..."* (John 4:21). Before worship can be initiated, it must begin with faith. She would move from being a lost Gentile to being included in the family of Abraham if she would apply faith at the outset. Everything about worship must be done from a position of faith if it is going to be counted as authentic. The Greek definition also means "to entrust (one's spiritual well-being)." This faith concern as it relates to worship presents a problem today in the context of what Jesus is asking the woman to do.

When I began to take golf seriously some years ago, I was constantly presented with this issue of trust. My coach would tell me to do a particular thing with my hands or with the club, and he would say, "Trust me." To entrust my swing's well-being to him was difficult only because it didn't feel right to me. He would always follow it up with, "I know it doesn't feel right, but trust me." When I would do as I was instructed and got a particular result, he would say, "See!" Arriving at that desired result always included an awkward feeling and trusting what I was told by someone who knew better.

What I describe in this book and part of what this woman was going through at the well is dependent in large part upon trust in what Christ is saying and not what we are used to. The worship being described will be awkward at first; it won't feel right because we have never done it this way before. However, it will produce the desired result. In swinging my own way, I would get hit-or-miss results, sometimes a good shot and most times not. When I did it the way my coach suggested, the results were more times than not successful, much to *my* surprise—but not his. What the Church will begin to experience more times than not is the desired result of His Presence in our midst as we worship in this new spiritual place.

Jesus continued in His answer with the phrase, *"The hour is coming..."* thus pointing to a future time of worship. This is the prophetic part of the answer that I believe the Church must receive. Jesus was giving us a clear picture of what worship would look like in the future, and we have misinterpreted it.

Worship was not to be left in our hands to shape and mold to our liking. The Father would not leave such an intricate and important part of our spiritual walk in our hands. So He insured that it will be carried forward under some very specific guidelines in His explanation to the woman. He knew that if it was left in our hands, it would get distorted over time. We would, as the woman had stated in her query, steer it toward things that have nothing to do with worship. Jesus, in His answer, set in motion classic standards for the future of worship, thereby removing the guesswork and, at the same time, ensuring that we will give the Father what He desires. So Jesus said the time would come when all worship will fit this classic criteria, and when this happens, the Father will be pleased with our worship. I believe that this time is now upon us.

We are presently in an era when worship varies widely from place to place, culture to culture, denomination to denomination, region to region, theological persuasion to theological persuasion, and so forth. If you consider yourself Pentecostal, you have one practice; if you're evangelical, you have another way; if you are contemporary, you have this preference; if you are traditional, you have that preference; if you are African American, you expect this; if you are Caucasian, you expect that. However, Jesus completely understands worship and desires to convey to anyone who is hungry an authentic worship context. Following His directive will satisfy the Father, and at the same time, we will find it satisfying to be participants in such an awesome experience.

The next era of worship will unify the Church in perspective and practice. It will lead us all to the same spiritual plateau. It will supersede our petty differences and override our theological persuasions.

It will have a tsunami effect on the Body of Christ as a whole; it will leave no one untouched. Some of what we have trusted in the past will be abandoned because the results will be so significantly dissimilar to what we will be experiencing. This will not only be meaningful for us, but undeniable for the world. The testimonies that will come out of this type of worship experience will be so extraordinary and will be solely contributed to the Presence that there will be no vain glory in the house of the Lord any longer.

Jesus' explanation of what worship will look like in the future is indeed an answer to a dilemma that has existed for over two thousand years. Yet the answer is as valid now as it was then. He further elaborated, "*...neither in this mountain nor in Jerusalem...,*" will be the focal point of worship. This took all parts of her query into consideration. Let's look at what He was saying closely.

In the woman's query, she highlighted four things that are of greatest concern in accomplishing authentic worship. Those four things are tradition, culture, location, and religion. Jesus' answer covered all four points in the two words *mountain* and *Jerusalem*. When He stated, "*...neither in this mountain...,*" He was taking on the issues of location and tradition. When He said, "*...nor in Jerusalem...,*" He was taking on the issues of culture and religion.

The mountain she was referring to is Mount Gerazim. The Samaritan traditions were limited to the Pentateuch, Abraham through Moses primarily (see Gen. 12:7; 33:18-20; Deut. 11:29; 27:12; Joshua 8:33). In the case of the Jews, they related their worship to Jerusalem or Mount Zion, based upon the deeds of David and Solomon. So the issue of where to worship was inclusive of location and tradition, which Jesus addressed when He referred to *mountain* in His answer.

Essentially, what Jesus was saying was that neither Jews nor Samaritans could claim infallible spiritual intelligence on the better location for authentic worship. If one group possessed a better location, it would essentially mean that the *where* of worship overrode the *who* of worship. This was probably shocking information to this Samaritan woman because she had most likely been taught that where she worshiped was paramount. In Jesus' answer, He did not defend His group nor did He exclusively condemn her group. This must have meant that Jesus possessed some information that superseded the earthly interpretation of worship completely. This particular approach is very rare today. As a matter of fact, all we tend to see from today's leaders is a defense of the group they represent, whether right or wrong. To see religious leaders neither defend their group nor condemn another is an anomaly.

However, what Jesus was really pointing to in making this statement was that, if worship was based purely upon exclusivity of location, the sincerity of worship would eventually deteriorate because humans tend to grow familiar with anything that does not include the heart. So even today, if worship only takes place in a church building, even if it is a new church building, the people will eventually take that location for granted, and the sincerity will wean over time. It also makes it too easy if it's only based upon location. That would mean that I could just show up and meet my spiritual obligation; this is true today also. When we look at the Old Testament, especially the temple era, we see this begin to manifest less than two generations from David. It didn't take long before the grandchild of David (Rehoboam) became indifferent to the temple that his grandfather had initiated and his father had built.

Still, there are deeper issues that Jesus was addressing here. The issue of racial divide in the midst of worship was plaguing that generation and is still prevalent today. Either of these locations caused another racial group to feel completely unwelcome, to the degree that they never cross-pollinated. How could worship be authentic if it made one racial group feel comfortable and another feel alienated? The problem with location worship is that it causes disunity, and disunity is not tolerated in the face of the Father. How is it that we could worship a Deity who made all of us, but only accepts some of us?

The other issue that should be raised about location worship is that it is short-sighted. One can only imagine the difficulty of all Christians being limited to one authentic location for worship. Since Christ envisioned thousands and thousands of people worshiping in the future, He knew that there would have to be a worship system instituted that would accommodate these thousands around the world in various locations. The system would encompass worship in any or many locations so as to allow worship to take place at anytime as long as the *who* of worship was not omitted.

It is fascinating to know that two religious/cultural groups could have had their traditions in tact based upon their forefathers' perspectives and yet not have the revelation of what the Father wanted. They had both based their positions on Scripture, they both felt like they were right and the other was wrong, yet they fostered division and perpetuated a false worship. All this and the confusion existed for probably more than two thousand years. Amazing! During this time, the people suffered from confusion and disillusionment, all because the leadership and the interpreters had it wrong. How long will we allow our religion and culture to cloud our obligation to worship the Father in Spirit and truth?

Obviously, Jesus' motivation was to bring this woman to a place where she could worship anywhere without restriction or limitation. He desired that she would be satisfied when she worshiped because she had touched Heaven. He wanted her to be free of something that had stumped Jews and Samaritans alike. He wanted her to walk in a dimension of worship where her questions could be answered and her heart could be put at ease. He wanted her to be a worshiper and not just go to a worship facility. This is what we need today now more than ever if there will be any integrity restored to the modern Church's corporate worship experience.

I agree with many of this generation who want to abandon the traditional worship that our Church fathers established hundreds of years ago. Many of the traditions had no biblical foundation, and

are snatching their influence and increasing in number. Very few authentic conversions are taking place; it is more of a reshuffling of the masses. We, like the Jews of Jesus' day, have become intoxicated with individuality. We have created these monuments to our own glory and spend time and money attracting people to them and not the Presence. Our headquarters are only truly recognized by our own constituents. The world ignores our so-called accomplishments for the most part. They don't understand why we do what we do, and they refuse to support our self-centered ventures.

Religion in this day is not what it used to be. It has very little respect from the culture. Recently, we've seen new challenges to anything and everything that has a religious connotation to it, and it will get worse as time goes by. The National Day of Prayer, In God We Trust, prayer in the congress and other state institutions, religious holidays such as Christmas and Easter and the like will be under more and more criticism as religion continues to lose its influence with the passing generations. The increase of terrorism by so-called Muslims and other religious sects will continue to serve one purpose in the world; that purpose, unbeknownst to many, is the diminishing of the need for participation in any religion.

Jesus' statement to the woman regarding worship and the future of worship was prophetic even to this generation in that religion and religious locations will neither be regarded nor hold their influence as they have in the past as this new worship standard is instituted. The new paradigm will render the old traditions irrelevant forever. What we once revered will now be looked at as weak and useless. It might be hard to digest at the moment, but most of what we see in the religious world today, whether it be from a Roman Catholic perspective or a non-denominational mega-church perspective, will become obsolete in the face of this new standard of worship. Once the authentic is revealed, everything else comes up short. It won't matter how old the institution is; it won't matter how well known the pastor is. It won't matter how much good they have done in the past; it won't even matter if they're influential over the entire globe. Once the authentic is revealed with its power and glory, the old, false, powerless systems will be ignored. The tsunami wave is close to the shore, and most Christians are completely unaware!

Now the complete statement of Christ found in verse 21 helps us to define where Jesus was going with His answer. He said, *"...Neither on this mountain, nor in Jerusalem, worship the Father"* (John 4:21). Jesus specifically included the Father in His answer, whereas the woman never mentioned the object of her worship. Her statement was ambiguous and assumptive; His was definitive.

Who we're worshiping must be identified so that we can identify with *Whom* we are worshiping. Her previous statement about worship did not do this specifically. We can either conclude that anyone listening to her talk would have known that she was talking about G-d, or we can conclude that she was talking about a god. Was she simply preoccupied with the practice of worship and not the person to whom the worship was directed? Was she so distracted by the location of worship that the focus of her worship had become secondary? Had she been so swept up in religion that she no longer engaged in relationship? Any of the scenarios may have been true for her and are true for many who worship in churches today.

The generic term *god* is used commonly by Christians and non-Christians, though Christians have many names for YHWH. The commonness of the name *god* could be the beginning of the worship problem. We have not given YHWH the distinction He deserves when referring to Him on Earth. That is why, throughout this book, I have not spelled out His name—out of respect for the common usage. This is similar to the way the Jews handle His name to this day. When I read between the lines of the woman's query, I can see that she was sincere in trying to realize authentic worship, yet her query did not focus on the object of her worship at all. If Jesus hadn't subtly addressed this then, He would have run the risk of having her leave His presence with satisfactory information about the religious practice, while still missing the principle purpose of worship, which is connecting with the Father.

So Jesus included in His answer the direction of worship when He said, *"...worship the Father."* He was specifically, according to the Greek word *pater,* stating who worship is directed toward so as to leave no ambiguity. *Pater* in the Greek means "Father." He could have used *theos* for "god," which is used later in verse 24, or He could have used *kurios* for "Lord" which He avoided completely in this discourse. It is clear that Jesus was making clear to the woman that there must be a relationship for worship to be authentic. The relationship that He highlighted by using *Father* makes clear that the worshiper comes from the One being worshiped. This makes identification a key component to worship.

Jesus does not use *Father* accidentally. When we look at the Father/child connotation, it is easy to see why He includes this in His answer. The father, even in the natural, brings identity to the family and to the children. Scripturally, fatherless children are spoken of as needing a covering, not motherless children. As a matter of fact, the word *motherless* is never used throughout the entire Bible, but the word *fatherless* is mention multiple times. If this woman was to worship effectively, it would be because she identified with the one *whom* she was worshiping. It is the father who determines the blood type and gender of the child. Jesus was saying that we can only worship the one whom we identify with, and the problem with worship at this time was identity. Neither Jews nor Gentiles were focusing on identifying with the Father; their worship was only identifying with traditions and locations, rendering it inauthentic. Relationship and identity are a prerequisite for authentic worship. Once this woman had turned to her heavenly Father and identified with Him through His Son, she would begin to move into a true worship experience. The issue of the Father being brought into the equation of worship is what justified the directness of Jesus' words in verse 22.

Verse 22 is one of the most direct slanders I have identified in Scripture to date (second to the Scripture in John 8:44 where Jesus calls the Jews' father the devil). If we really look at what Jesus said, there is no way we can sidestep the uncompromising directness of His comment. *"You worship what you do not know...,"* is a very clear slander of the Gentile worship practice. You can't be more direct than that! Jesus told this poor woman to her face that she had no idea what worship was about because she was outside of the family to whom worship had been introduced. Wow! That is exactly the way I feel about what is being promoted as worship today, especially in America. We spend millions of dollars on marketing a worship style or concept, and we send it around the world, not realizing that we have no idea what we are doing. We email our prophecies and tweet our Scripture lessons and stream our worship services as if we are pleasing the Father. And Jesus said to the Gentile, obviously you have no idea what this is all about.

This is the frightening reality that got my attention when the Lord started dealing with me about the worship at TWC. We were simply doing what we had been doing. Then we were doing what I thought we should be doing. Then we started doing what the Father desired we do. It's still amazing to me that I have been going to churches all of my life, was raised in the Church, and was groomed in ministry, yet had no clue as to what the Father expected when I entered His house. All I was familiar with was "having a good service" and making sure the excitement and emotion was high.

As a Gentile-thinking Christian, disconnected from my Hebraic roots, I had moved from one extreme to the next. I have dressed up and dressed down. I have preached for twenty minutes and one-and-a-half hours. I've used a program and discarded the program. I've gone from singing hymns and spirituals to singing worship music written by myself and others; I've gone from demanding offerings to not even mentioning money, from altar calls twice a service to no altar calls at all, from anniversaries and human-made holidays to the biblical feasts of Israel. You name it, and I've done it. All the while, I was attempting to figure this thing out called *worship*. With all of this under my belt, it has only been over the past several years that I have made the connection back to the Hebraic roots of Scripture that have brought me to the reality of my faith and the authenticity of my worship. Without this connection, I am grappling in the dark, hoping to come across something that strikes a chord with others and creates another trend that is short-lived.

Gentile worship is ineffectual. It's contemporary. It lacks foundation. It lacks identity. It's entertainment. It's pleasing to people and not to the Father. It's religion. It's cultural. It's unsatisfying. It's hit-or-miss. It's frustrating. It's void of the shekinah. It's dying.

Dealing with this statement from Jesus is like looking at the previous forty years of my own worship experiences and writing them off as a colossal mishap. Yes, there were times when I felt like we were genuinely being ministered to by the Holy Spirit, no doubt. Yes, there were times when we fell on our faces and worshiped the Father in spirit and in truth. Sure there were times when we received a sure word of revelation. Additionally, there were times of authentic healing and deliverance. However, the problem was that there was no true connection of consistency and authenticity that could be perpetuated the next time we gathered. It was looked at as an event that passed and could not be recaptured. There was no definitive scriptural formula or worship validity that went along with it. We simply hoped in vain that we could have that glory meet us again, and in fact, it very seldom happened that way.

The truth is, we had no idea what we were engaging in. We thought it was the song or the sermon. We thought it was the fast or fervor. We, in many cases, thought it was the day, such as Pentecost Sunday, Good Friday, or Easter Sunday. We thought it was the event, such as the revival, the seminar, the all-night prayer meeting, the annual convocation, or something like that. Still, more than anything else, we truly believe to this day that it is the preacher, prophet, bishop, evangelist, pastor, or celebrity. This is still the driving force behind most of what we have deemed powerful ministry or extraordinary worship services. You can tell because everyone leaves the service giving credit to that person for the experience and not the Holy Spirit. What an unfortunate reality that we have arrived at after two thousand plus years; we are still confused about who deserves the glory for an unusual outpouring in a meeting. Again, it is only because Gentiles have no idea what worship is all about.

The more biblical perspective of this statement is that Jesus was saying that it is impossible for Gentiles to be versed in worship and know what the Father expects when worship was not given to them from the beginning. In order for Gentiles to be successful in worship, as this Samaritan woman was attempting to do, they would first have to have some type of introduction to what began with Abraham and was crystallized with Moses and transcended to David. If that didn't happen, there was no way of coming close to understanding not only the act of worship, but also the process whereby worship is deemed authentic.

I can remember teaching a curriculum I developed called the "Hebraic Connection to Our Faith" at a couple of Bible institutes in New York City. I would always start off the first class the same way. I would ask the students what they thought the class would be about or what they expected to learn while in the class, and the answers would vary in several ways. Then I would warn them that the class was going to shake up their theology entirely and, with that in mind, they were welcome to leave before the class got started. Then I would tell them that they might get upset with their present ministry and leadership after they digested the first couple of classes. At that point, I would get looks of disbelief or attitude (like, *Who does this guy think he is?*). Then I would tell them that the main thing that they would understand from the class is that the Christianity that they are practicing is entirely Gentile and, therefore, cannot be trusted to satisfy the longing of their hearts, but only frustrate it.

By this time, everyone would be so anxious, but curious that they didn't know what to do. Then I would give them an example of what I was referring to with these absurd and over-the-top comments. I would invite them to turn to Matthew 6:23 and read it. I would give them a moment to think about it, and then I would ask them to explain what they had just read. (This was normally where it got good.) There were always a few who dared not to answer and a few who knew exactly what they thought this Scripture is about. I would get answers like, "It is about a keeping oneself from evil," or "It is about casting a spell on someone," or "It is a picture of someone who is not saved," as well as other much crazier answers. Then I would ask them to look at the context a little closer and see if there are any clues as to what this verse might be about. That was typically when the room filled with puzzled and curious faces that realize they may be very wrong in their interpretations, though they have nothing new to offer.

It was at this point that I would relieve them of their stress by explaining first that the Scripture could not be interpreted accurately unless you have a Jewish background, since the verse uses a Jewish nuance. With this in mind, I would ask them if they knew what *"manga-manga"* means if they were sitting at a table with Italians getting ready to eat? Of course, they would take a guess at this, and some would come close to the right answer. Then I would state that the way they guessed about this Italian term is the same way that they have guessed about the interpretation of this Scripture. The only problem is that most of them would teach it to others based upon their supposition and not accuracy, and that is the very problem facing Gentile Christianity today; we are guessing instead of knowing.

This simple example is the main reason why I believe Gentile worship misses the mark. There is no foundational connection to our Hebraic roots (see Rom. 11), which makes it necessary to begin to understand what the Father desires from His children in corporate worship. If we fail to see this, we run the risk of doing things that seem right, but could be so far from sufficient that the exposure of such could cause a revolt. While we are doing things that are exciting and contemporary and attractive to the masses, it could be the polar opposite of what we should be doing. Yet due to our visible success, no one will ever ask the question, "Is this authentic and pleasing to Father based upon His prerequisites or not?"

I recall hearing three of our most highly-regarded celebrity preachers within the space of about a month all refer to the same Old Testament story of Cain and Abel. These men, who will remain nameless, have some of the largest churches in the country, have widely viewed television programs, and are noted authors. With these accomplishments to their credit, most would believe their interpretations to be accurate and true. Yet they all used the story of Cain and Abel to refer to bringing G-d your best in one way or another. They each had similar interpretations of the reason why Cain's offering was rejected, and it amazed me how one can be so wrong and so sincere at the same time; I know because I've been there. If they had a Hebraic foundation, they would have been able to properly interpret from a scriptural context why Cain's offering was rejected and why Abel's was accepted. Once I shared this explanation with someone who had never heard it before, and they just about called me a heretic. Their reason: They had never heard anyone say it before; that's all.

Nevertheless, it is clear from the preceding chapter that G-d had already set the precedent for how to please Him in sacrifice with Adam and Eve. The Scripture says plainly that G-d made *"coats of skin"* for Adam and Eve after their failure. The coats of skin came off of the bodies of innocent animals, which G-d had to slay in order to save Adam and Eve from His wrath. With this context, Adam must have continued with some form of regularity the practice of slaying an innocent animal every time (or periodically) he came before the Father. This practice was continued before Cain and Abel to the extent that the Scripture says in Genesis 4:3 that in the *"process of time,"* meaning "when Cain and Abel had become accountable for their own worship." What this means from a Hebraic perspective is that they had moved past the age of accountability (age twelve or thirteen). They were now of an age where, after watching their parents perform worship, they could perform it for themselves. They knew what was expected and acceptable.

Abel did what he knew was acceptable; he brought an offering with *blood* in it. Cain ignored what he knew was the only acceptable practice, and he brought something that was bloodless. It's a very simple interpretation. It has nothing to do with bringing the *"best,"* as many Gentile preachers have loudly declared. It has to do with giving the Father what He demands, not what we prefer. But without a Hebraic understanding of the entire context, Gentiles will pull from this text what they feel sounds good and promote it as truth; this is not good!

So this is the challenge. Returning to our Hebraic roots becomes as essential for us as it would be for this seeking Samaritan. Not returning means we are convinced beyond any question that what we are practicing is completely accurate and above criticism. Yet at the same time, I submit that even a brief overview of the history of the Christian Church will reveal at a glance that we got off the mark some 1,800 years ago and have been straying ever so slightly since that time. That would mean that 1,800 years later, we are way off course and are in need of a dramatic shift in direction if we are to begin to move back toward original intent. But of course, this would call for unprecedented humility and an admission of error. Yet in the midst of this crisis of unsatisfactory, mundane, predictable, redundant worship, I am completely confident that a tsunami of change is just a few divine moments away and that everything will change in days to come anyway. The issue of becoming Hebraic in our approach to the Christian faith is foundational to our ability to please the Father in worship and service to the kingdom.

The indictment of Christ upon the Gentile worshiper has to be taken seriously. We have to ask ourselves the really tough questions about what we practice and what we have been advocating as authentic worship. Do we give the Father a Sabbath? Do we lock Him in to a timeframe in which He must move? Do we promote people as idols in the midst of worship? Have we distorted and contaminated the worship sanctuary with our secular humanist worldview? Do we practice scriptural holy days or secular holidays? Do we worship the Lord in giving or shakedown the people with ulterior motives? Are our ministry structures biblical or just traditionally compliant? Do we advocate the kingdom of G-d active here on Earth, or are we simply setting up our own kingdoms to serve our own purposes? Do we seek to affect the head or affect the heart?

There are a thousand more of these questions that probe the thin line between ministry and ministering to the Father that need to be considered. They are tough questions, but they all stem from taking Jesus' comment seriously: *Do we have any idea what we are doing?* Admitting that I was clueless was my first step in the right direction when the Lord began to deal with me along the lines of church ministry and corporate worship.

Galatians 4:5 speaks of an adoption that has taken place with those who have now become heirs with Christ. This issue of adoption must be taken seriously in that in Christ we are indeed a part of a new family. Even in the natural, when someone of age is adopted, that person has to go through a period of adjusting to the culture of the new family. This person is the same person, having the same personality and characteristics and the same first name. However, because of that adoption, this person has to begin to understand the rules and culture of the new family, learning the language and nuances of that new family in order to be successful in communicating with the family leadership. What the Gentile Church has completely omitted in its attempt to make disciples is introducing new Gentile believers to the new family's roots. So we have raised up a group of Christians who have remained *"the wild olive branch"* though they were supposed to be grafted into the cultivated olive tree (see Rom. 11). As such, we have been given a Christian religion that looks, acts, and talks like it's a part of the family of Abraham, but in truth is far from it. Without a true adoption, we will continue to worship what we do not know (see John 4:22).

Jesus makes it very clear and emphatic, without apology, that *salvation* or the introduction to relationship and worship of the Father is of the Jews, not the Gentiles. In this, He takes personal ownership for worship, even though the nation of Israel had not done a good job with it. He dealt with the fact that remains. Israel had strayed, but it didn't change YHWH's original intent when He introduced Himself to Abraham and told Him that He would have a people from his loins if he would just believe. That relationship with Abraham was the beginning of what G-d would perform throughout many generations and thousands of years in spite of Israel's inconsistency. He would introduce His plans for a land to be called His, deliverers who would bring this people out, commandments and special memorials, the tabernacle and temple, the Ark of His presence, signs and wonders—all so that this people of all peoples would know what He required in worship and relationship with Him.

He did this with no other group, just the Hebrews. He engaged with them and made sure that there would be an eternal book to document His relating to them over thousands of years with stories on top of stories, all because this was the group through which His plans in the Earth would be revealed and executed. No other nation has this history, this continuity, this rich and abiding tradition with YHWH. Therefore, Jesus need not apologize when belittling the efforts of this Gentile in worship; worship is indeed of the Jews.

Does this mean that every Gentile Christian needs to become Jewish? Yes! However, it is imperative that we don't confuse the Jew of this day with what I am referring to. Neither should we confuse the process of becoming Jewish. Whenever I deal with this issue, I am questioned as to what this will look like. I am very careful to note that my reference point for becoming Hebraic is found in the Scriptures and in the words of our Jewish leader. I am not talking about the modern twenty-first century Jews. I am not even talking about the Jews of recent history, who may have been as far off in their faith as we are in ours. I'm talking about getting new insight about what was given to Abraham, Isaac, and Jacob—taking a fresh look at what was carried forward by Joseph, handed off to Moses, and fulfilled in Joshua—about looking at what David instituted and what Solomon established, about looking at what the prophets propagated and how Jesus completed it. This reexamination will be necessary for us to begin to move into what is truly Hebraic and allow us to become one with the cultivated olive tree. This is why at TWC we refer to ourselves as a Judeo-Christian ministry. Our roots are Jewish, and we must become comfortable with our new family if we are ever going to be one with them.

I am not referring to this substitutional or replacement theology that is going around. I do not refer here to taking the place of Jews; Romans 11:17-21 clearly outlines the foolishness of such a concept. However, being adopted or grafted in is surely what I believe every Christian has to accept as an essential part of the faith. This grafting in comes with our acceptance and belief in Jesus Christ. If we reject this, we continue to function from notions and creativity concerning worship and Christianity that falls in the context of trends, opinions, and the contemporary. We have a history of this already, and the results of those practices have led us to an Ezekiel 37-type existence; the Church has become nothing more than dry bones scattered about. I contend that we take heed to the words of Jesus our Jewish Messiah and acknowledge our ignorance of the Hebraic approach to Scripture and its impact upon our practices.

What I admire most about this Samaritan woman is similar to my admiration of the Canaanite woman in Matthew 15. After receiving what could be considered offensive responses from Christ, neither of them got an attitude and walked away. In both cases, they allowed their pursuit of deliverance to take priority over any disparaging statements that Jesus made to them. Many people who read this book may take offense at some of the things written herein; however, those who have a dominate pursuit of deliverance from their present situation will continue to read to consider the entirety of this presentation. With all that had been presented to this Samaritan woman, she remained constant. She had been uncharacteristically approached by a Jewish man, she had been given a parable about water, she had been given unfamiliar information about worship, she had been told about her personal life, and now she was being informed that Gentiles had no idea what worship was about—yet she was still engaged with Jesus, unmoved.

Since she had withstood all of this, Jesus finally gave her the secret of authentic worship. He began with two contexts of thought that are difficult for those in the natural to receive. He talked to her about the timing of the dimension of worship that she sought and when it would be revealed. In stating, *"The hour is coming, and now is..."* (John 4:23), Jesus presented what, on the outside, looked like a confusing timeframe. *"The hour is coming"* was the timing for the world based upon His death and resurrection and when He would be lifted up and revealed as the Savior. The *"now"* was for the woman who was getting her personal revelation of the Savior. Thus, her worship would change immediately; she did not have to wait for the crucifixion and resurrection.

This is significant, even in today's modern worship experience. For some, they will not understand what is being said in this book until the return of Christ or what is revealed in the Book of Revelation starts to manifest. For others, the hour is now because they realize that this is the missing link to what they have been waiting for and what they see in churches today and in corporate worship. The need for the shift in worship is dire, and they will make their move without delay. This phrase also embodies the dimension that

Jesus functioned in all the time. He was subject to time in the Earth realm; however, He was well aware of the timeless nature of the Father in the heavenly realm. In that realm, everything was already done; in the Earth realm, those same things had a timeframe for manifestation. This allows the woman to immediately move into a new dimension of worship and not wait for all of the other components to be in place before she could enjoy what her soul longed for.

In the balance of verse 23, Jesus continued by describing what the Father (again Father, not G-d) desires, and this gives a graphic picture of the Father's position as it relates to the worship that He receives. The Father is *"seeking"* a particular type of worshiper to satisfy Him. This worshiper worships in *"spirit and truth."* With this description of what the Father is seeking, there should be no discrepancy or misunderstanding as to what we should be presenting every time we gather for a corporate worship celebration. But is this what we experience in our churches? Do we recognize or sense an atmosphere where everyone is concerned with the Father being pleased and satisfied by our worship? I don't think so. As a matter of fact, the dominate notion today is that we should make the atmosphere as conducive to the "seeker" and not the One being sought. Everything is designed so that the worshiper or seeker is being accommodated and made to feel comfortable more than the One to whom the worship is directed.

How did we come to such a notion? Very simple, it's a Gentile concept. The Gentile approach to worship will continue to come up with things that are not scriptural and that are counter-Hebraic in that they simply don't line up with all that has been previously established as acceptable. And in this case, just like Cain, most of our worship is being rejected because we are giving G-d what we came up with and not what He has established. Most of today's Church atmospheres are totally and completely designed and crafted to "minister" to the people. We want the people to go home feeling warm and fuzzy, we want them to come back again next Sunday, and G-d knows we want them to bring their pocketbooks. We don't want to offend them, we don't want to keep them too long, we don't want to challenge them in the wrong way, and we don't even want to talk about their sin anymore. We just want them to think that church is wonderful and that they should want to have this wonderful and loving G-d in their lives. This is the new presentation of the Church and its worship experiences.

We have forgotten the origin of corporate worship, according to Exodus 25:8, which says, *"Make **Me** a sanctuary that I may dwell among them,"* not, "Make for yourselves a church building that I can visit whenever you invite Me." Whether it was the enemy or just our Gentile thinking, the entire worship experience and environment has been turned about almost to the degree that we can call the whole thing a perversion of the original. YHWH is seeking worshipers! So how is it that we have now twisted worship so that people are seeking? This is a fascinating misdirection of the centrality of worship. If we create a seeker-sensitive environment, we actually make the seeker the center of our focus. This is a secular humanist approach to worship, and it does not meet the mandate that Jesus clarified for the Samaritan woman. The Father is seeking worshipers who come before His Presence in spirit and truth!

So how do we begin to move toward this kind of acceptable worship, and what does it look like? Well, we have to begin with the understanding that spirit must equate to authenticity, and truth must equate to accuracy. Throughout the Scriptures, we can always see the clear connection between the spirit (whether the Holy Spirit or human spirit) and the only reliable way of measuring spiritual authenticity. This is clearly why the Bible says in First Corinthians 2:10-11:

> *But God has revealed them to us through His Spirit. For the Spirit searches all things, yes, the deep things of God. For what man knows the things of a man except the spirit of the*

man which is in him? Even so no one knows the things of God except the Spirit of God.

Everything is authentic in the spirit realm. Things in the natural are often disguised or misrepresented, but in the realm of the spirit, there is no distortion of the authentic. It is the realm of G-d; it is the realm of the truly genuine. It is in this realm that the Father desires to meet with us—not on our terms, not under our preconditions, not based on our convenience or comfort. The Father says that if we meet Him in this realm, everything we present to Him will be legitimate, legal, authentic, genuine, valid, and so forth. Nothing will be tainted with humanistic motivations or perverse perspectives, which are not acceptable in the Presence of the Lord.

In my estimation, the authentic is impossible to accomplish with any type of consistency as long as our approach, our leaders, our liturgies, our music, our atmosphere, our environment, and our church designs are without the high and holy spiritual mandate expressed through the Scriptures. What is authentic is expressed through the spirit of the letter, and if this is ignored based upon our dis-ease with its mandates, we will continue to fail to reach the "spirit" of worship. Authenticity is not based upon what we make up and stick to for four hundred years; this just makes us authentically wrong. What we need when it comes to authenticity is the ability to receive revelation of what the Father wants based upon what He has written in the volume of the Book. Our authenticity is typically compared to the things that we have seen in recent history. In most cases, this is a bad comparison and only brings about alternatives, not authenticity. This is why we have gone from hymns to hip-hop and heavy metal right in the midst of worship. We are always thinking in terms of alternatives and not the authentic. So the Father is seeking and accepting authentic worshipers who approach Him the only way He can be touched—in the spirit realm. To present anything else to Him is basically objectionable, yet this is what most of our worship looks like when it reaches Him: unacceptable.

So the local church can do a number of things that inspire the worshipers and make them feel more like they are entering into a place of deeper spirituality; however, it will most likely be related to emotionalism or religion. Without the spirit or the authenticity of what is revealed by the Father through His Word being applied, the experience will fail to meet the standard Jesus outlined in this text. It has nothing to do with the talent of the preacher, the skill of the musicians and singers, the expertise of the leadership, or the contemporary awareness of the ministry; this is about meeting G-d in His realm, the realm of the spirit. Furthermore, all of the other inspirational things that we have relied on in the past lose their pre-eminence in the light of a spirit experience. So it is imperative that we worship YHWH in spirit.

Still, we must not forget the aspect of truth or accuracy that is mandated as the counterpart to the spirit. Jesus said spirit-and-truth worshipers are being *sought* by the Father. The aspect of truth must be dealt with in this truth-less generation. We are so used to half truths and diluted truth (which in reality are not truth at all) that we have developed an acceptance for it rather than demanded truth at all cost.

Truth is very easily equated to accuracy throughout the Scriptures. Jesus said, *"You shall know the truth..."* (John 8:32). Once accurate information is exposed, we are automatically delivered from ignorance. The only acceptable worship is worship that is practiced in accuracy (correctness/exactness). The Father has the right to demand this since He left a document to describe for us exactly what He wants; therefore, there is no excuse for giving Him anything less. This is seen in the Cain situation in Genesis, and it has carried forward, much to our ignorance, ever since. Somehow over the years, we have become so self-centered in ministry and worship until it seems we have truly forgotten that the Father never left the standards of worship to us. He has always made it clear to every one of His leaders exactly what He wants. In this, we have but one obligation—follow

His instructions. This is why He says to Saul that obedience is better than sacrifice. It has always been YHWH's preference that we (His creation) follow His instructions as an act of obedience (since He may want different things under different circumstances), and it will satisfy Him more so than giving a robotic sacrifice.

Worship services have fallen into the category of sacrifice. We simply do what we know to do and not what we are asked to do. In this, many feel like they have accomplished worship when really they've only met their religious quota for the week. Meeting the quota becomes robotic for us as Old Testament sacrifice did for the Israelites. After a while, the heart is not even involved in the process; we just go through the motions. Sometimes there is a little more emotion involved, and that is so often mistaken for spirituality that we think we went to a new level because we were crying or screaming loudly. Yet in fact, it was nothing more than an emotional religious exercise. We must conform to the standard that has been prescribed as accurate via the Scriptures.

Now it will be very easy for people to misinterpret this as being unnecessarily critical or for others to form a theological debate about accurate interpretation of Scripture. In either case, that is not the purpose of using such direct language as it relates to accurate worship. I am mindful that there are a million and one ministry leaders who use Scripture erroneously every week. There are even more who are simply so defensive that any type of criticism is mishandled as a religious attack from another Christian. However, it is more valuable to look at the queries presented by the Samaritan woman that I have outlined and look at the answers Jesus gave as our guideline to understand how we have missed the mark and have become terribly inaccurate in the way that we have presented and described worship for the masses.

Accuracy in this case is not limited to the interpretation of one or two Scriptures or a few theological views. Accuracy based upon how Jesus responded has much more to do with understanding what was shown to Adam and Eve, what was handed to the Hebrews at the beginning of corporate worship, and how it transcended to the point at which G-d Himself commented that what He gave David in worship would be restored in the last days. If the understanding of worship is based upon what was given to the Jews, it would be examined from that perspective, and the inaccuracy of worship we see today would be eradicated without prejudicial theological arguments or secularly driven scriptural interpretations.

The way I generally view Gentile worship is like having a compass that is magnetically flawed; if you don't know that it is fundamentally flawed, then you will follow the north pointer as if it is accurate, and you will be sincerely wrong. It reminds me of the time the Lord showed me that the Church was like the Leaning Tower of Pisa. The tower itself is not really the problem; it is the foundation that caused the tower to lean. He further showed me that the Church has chosen not to deal with the foundation. Instead, we have decided to make it a visitor's attraction, and just like in the case of the tower, we make money by exhibiting our flaws and masquerading them as a wonder worthy of an audience. We have done it so well that no one dares ask, "What is wrong with the foundation?"

We need ministry that is accurate in order to enter the awesome Presence. This accuracy is based upon a truthful revelation of what G-d wants and expects from His creation when they approach Him in worship. Ministry must provide this information to the community of believers, regardless of how it may undermine what we have done over the last one hundred or one thousand years or what we have been saying to people throughout our ministry. Accuracy often means we have to rescind something we have said previously or that we have to apologize for how we may have misinterpreted a Scripture in the past. This takes a monumental amount of humility, and often ministry leaders aren't willing to be called wrong in this day and age.

Accuracy in my estimation will deal with the deepest and dearest practices of the modern Church. It will expose our unbiblical church hierarchy and structures. It will expose our stale and antiquated liturgies. It will demand the dissolution of denominations (divisions) in the Body of Christ. It will beg for the reexamination of four hundred-year-old plus theological opinions. It will decry the strange fire (secular music) that we have offered in holy worship. It will invoke the guidance of the invisible leader of the Church—the Holy Spirit. It will require a fresh revelation of the kingdom of G-d and its purpose in the earth. It will necessitate that we seriously consider the sanctuary design that we have sanctioned versus the one that YHWH left in Scripture as the pattern for His house. It will warrant an agreement with Hebraic thinking according to and in sync with our Jewish leader. It will stipulate that the only one to be entertained by our actions is the Father of Glory and not people. These are just the beginnings of what it will take to move into a more accurate and authentic worship experience in the last day.

Since G-d is the epitome of authenticity in every regard, we must submit to the method by which we, as mere human beings, can interact with the authentic. It is such an awesome privilege to be participants in worship that we should be honored to hold court with the King under whatever stipulations He may demand. Coming into the Presence of the King of the universe should have stipulations. Coming into the presence of the President of the United States or the Queen of England or the King of Jordan has stipulations, so why wouldn't we be willing to submit to the stipulations of El Shaddai? I view myself as so ignorant concerning the meticulous desires of such an awesome and esteemed G-d that I need Him to outline the guidelines so that I don't invoke His wrath upon my entrance into His Presence.

G-d is a Spirit, the Scripture says. He made me out of Himself in such a way that I, in a very small way, represent Him in this earthly container. So in essence, He is calling me to present the most authentic part of my being back to Him for true fellowship. He doesn't want me to present my corrupted and corroded flesh, nor does He desire my wayward and distracted soul; He desires that part of me which best represents Himself, my spirit. In a way that I am not completely able to articulate, the Father simply desires to fellowship with an element of Himself in me. This would mean that the most satisfying worship experience for G-d would be the one where He is able to connect with Himself in me and defy the enemy and the flesh who want to circumvent this fellowship. This is why the devil loves to see us in the flesh and in our emotions during worship. He knows that this makes no connection with the Father.

By the time Jesus finished, the Samaritan was fully convinced that the prophet with whom she was speaking had sufficiently prepared her for an even greater experience with the Messiah when He finally came on the scene. This opened the door for Christ to expose who He was directly. Once He made clear to her that He was the Messiah, the woman realized that she had just had a face-to-face experience with G-d. She had received the reward of worship—to be found in the Presence. Not only was she found in His Presence, but also she had her deepest questions answered, which is the byproduct of worship. Once the revelation of Christ was made clear, the Father revealed Himself intimately and personally to the worshiper. The barrier was removed, and the glory was revealed. Isn't that what we come to worship for? Isn't this the ultimate reason for our gatherings, large and small? Not to see a choir or a preacher? Not to see or be seen? Not to entertain or display our flesh? The reason for our gatherings is to be in the Presence of the Almighty and to have our questions answered.

Unfortunately, today, modern ministry's success stories are not centered on this concept. We have subtly yet spiritually transformed the environment of worship to a setting where some spiritual people are on display, providing the entertainment for a worship service. Some do it better than others, and for that reason they become successful from a worldly perspective. Yet in the case of Jesus and the Samaritan woman, the goal of the experience was simple and concise—coming face-to-face with the Master, having her deepest queries answered, and leaving as a different person. For the Samaritan woman, the transformation was obvious. She had indeed accepted Him as the Messiah, and this was signified in her departure from the well without her water pot and her evangelism to the men of her town concerning her experience.

This New Testament encounter with Christ is one of the most significant and important passages concerning worship in the modern age. It deals with the difficulties that we face today and settles age-old arguments about worship. An acceptance of Jesus' responses to the woman should be viewed as applicable to today's corporate worship and should foster change for the Body of Christ in this area.

CHAPTER 11

APPLYING HEAVENLY ATTRIBUTES TO OUR EARTHLY WORSHIP

By now you should be experiencing some radically different thoughts and paradigm shifts in your views of corporate worship. I emphasize again that the focus here is not on personal worship that may take place in the privacy of your home or a small group setting. The spotlight is on correcting what has become known as the "church service" and more recently the "worship service" in the modern Church experience. How we enter the sanctuary, what it looks like, what we expect to experience, and how we carry it out is the issue of this book. Moving away from the redundancy of the liturgy, the spectatorship, entertainment, emotion-driven, and personality-driven environment is really what we have been dealing with throughout these chapters.

If we are willing to depart from these practices, and I believe most of us are by this point, then we need to know what to expect and how to prepare for this next era of worship. The future of worship is going to be wrapped around one overwhelming reality and that is the manifest Presence and coming face-to-face with the sheki-nah. It will not be anything like what we have been experiencing, even on our best days of worship. It will be difficult and uncomfortable for some people to even grasp this at first because the habits and practices of the past are so deeply engrained. However, it will be from that plateau that we will make the transition.

It will feel somewhat like the experience that Isaiah had in the year Uzziah died (see Isa. 6). Isaiah was not aware of it before this momentous experience, but he was lacking divine revelation in his life. However, it was in the year that Uzziah died, or in the year that the human influence was removed, that he began receiving divine revelation. It will be difficult to make this transition because we have put our leaders in such idolatrous places in our psyches that it feels awkward or sacrilegious to remove them from those places. Yet for Isaiah, it was an essential bridge to cross in order to change the direction of his affection and receive his spiritual impartation.

This is not to suggest that *all* leadership holds an idolatrous place in our spiritual experience, but in many cases they do. In many cases, it's not even the fault of the follower or the leader; it is simply the culmination of not taming the beast called the flesh over many hundreds of years. The difficulty is in admitting it and then giving the triune G-d that preeminence and allowing the human leader to serve the purpose that Scripture has outlined without the glory being shared in your mind or in reality. If we don't actively move these leaders out of our psyche, then it will leave the Father no choice but to diminish them in His own way. Some leaders nowadays actually try to be a god to their followers; others simply knowingly share the glory, which in either case sets them up for removal, as in the case of Uzziah in Isaiah's eyes.

Once Isaiah saw the Lord, there was an obvious distinction between what he was seeing presently and what he had seen in the past. People can never and will never be greater than the Almighty. However, when our eyes are not truly trained on the Creator, we tend to think that the created is great and awesome in leadership. Yet in the case of Isaiah, as will be in the case of many saints today, we will see the Lord *"sitting on a throne,"* which will be a clear indication that He has reclaimed the place that we have given to human leadership over these many thousands of years. We will recognize that He is *"high and lifted up"* in a place where we have never seen the human leader, a place the human leader could never attain through natural accomplishments. We will see the Lord in an exclusive place that only He can ascend to in our eyes and hearts. This will be further exacerbated by *"His train filling the temple"* and thus exposing the sheer greatness of His conquest over every other king. Though in the past we have celebrated (annually in most cases) the conquest of our human leadership with great words of laud and honor, we will understand that this King's accomplishments prove His superiority and dominion over *all* of His enemies. For Isaiah, this must have been truly significant since he was obviously aware of Uzziah's triumphs and victories. However, in this case, there was no comparison to Adonai. For us, this would mean that there is no space or place to mention what we have done in light of what He has done on His own without our assistance. To sustain temple worship, the focus must be on who Adonai is and what He has done. Our accomplishments fade quickly and cannot sustain the momentum of the temple.

This overwhelming sense of the greatness of our G-d is what worship should look like. We the leadership should deflect most recognition based upon the fact that we know, above all, that we are, at best, flawed camouflages of human beings whose dark side is always lurking in the shadows. Any and all of the great leaders throughout the Bible were not only exposed for this fact, but also functioned from an acute awareness of this reality. Peter, in this light, is said to have not felt worthy to die the same way that his Christ died; therefore, it was his preference to be upside down during his crucifixion. We must have an environment that is preoccupied with the great and awesome presence of Adonai, and this will be most notable by the decline of the praise and celebration of human leadership. He will not share His glory with another!

Isaiah's experience was transformational; he could not remain the same person after having viewed the Lord in this light. This is what we should be experiencing in our worship. He saw the King being worshiped in a way he had never seen Uzziah honored. Isaiah 6:2-3 says that he saw the six winged seraphim flying around with covered faces and feet. This signifies the great reverence and respect that even the spiritual beings have for the Almighty. Their holy cries highlight the superlative nature of His holiness—highest admiration, highest esteem, and over-exaggerated praise. No one can compare to Him. Obviously, this praise and worship has nothing to do with the beings and everything to do with the King. The Earth being filled with His glory means that everything speaks of Him.

This type of heavenly worship produces emphatic and dramatic results. What happened to Isaiah will happen to us when we enter into this dimension of worship. It will immediately generate self-examination and environmental assessment. Then the comparison of what is worthy is directed toward the King and not the flesh, which means that no humans could be found worthy (on their own) of being in His Presence. Isaiah's assessment is that he and all who are around him are unfit to be in the Presence of the King. It is only under these circumstances of humility that the Lord will move quickly and graciously to remove the impurities from our hearts and prepare us for kingdom usage. With this, we are made ready to participate in kingdom assignments without confusing those assignments with some special or superior spiritual positioning that in turn taints the work He has given us to do.

Whenever we see heavenly worship in the Scriptures, it should cause us to see what the expectation of worship really is. We must take these heavenly attributes and apply them to our earthly expressions to move closer to what is authentic and true. We can see those types of overwhelming and extraordinary experiences in Revelation

1:10-17 with John on the Isle of Patmos. He was worshiping in the Spirit on the Lord's Day, and it opened him up to the greatest experience and revelation of his lifetime. Later in chapter 4, the result of his worship is a *"door standing open,"* which is a clear sign that his worship gave him access. This heavenly attribute must become a part of our earthly worship in that we gain spiritual access through our worship experiences. In the natural sense, we just worship and move on to other things that are planned for that day. In the heavenly context, our worship should bring us to an access point that gives us further entry to deeper revelation. In John's case, the revelation was about the One who sat on the throne. What is more needed in today's Church than that? A Spirit revelation of the Father is the Body of Christ's greatest need. We have reduced the Father and boxed Him into a corner and made Him the great magician in the sky who must come to our rescue whenever we call, supplying our every want and need.

The picture of worship that is revealed to John in this passage was sure to change John's perspective of worship forever. He sees the living creatures, the twenty-four elders, the crowns of gold, the lightning and thunder, the voices, the lamps of fire, the rainbow, the sea of glass, the noise, and the cry of "holy, holy, holy!" This heavenly depiction must have opened John up to what worship should really be about in the Earth realm. This is what is needed today. We don't need a new façade or a new children's wing; we don't need a larger choir or a new pastor; we don't need more money or more fame; we don't need another revival or awakening; we simply need to worship with a heavenly perspective. We need a revelation of what worship encompasses and how to please the Father in every aspect of that experience. This must and will become the driving force of every ministry that recognizes that we have failed in this area. We must become consumed as the beasts and the elders are with who G-d is—absorbing His presence and becoming like Him in the process. Nothing less than this type of corporate experience will be acceptable.

Every time we see people enter into this type of worship in the Bible, it has produced dramatic and extraordinary manifestation in the lives of the worshipers. You can name them, from Abraham on down to John on the Isle of Patmos. Each of them has these unimaginable worship manifestations that literally change the course of history for the kingdom's sake. Yet we have reduced worship to an hour and a half so that we can either get the next group in or simply go on about our day, and each time we do that, we are cheating ourselves and disrespecting our Father, the Lord Jesus Christ, and the Holy Spirit. If and when we are finally able to break free, we will enter into another dimension, and we will never go back to that practice again.

We should expect timeless worship, not timed worship. It doesn't have to last all day, but it should not be locked into a timeframe. In other words, let the Lord dictate in His house what He desires for that season. We should expect holy music to emerge and not culturally driven, trendy music composed or based on popular sounds. There is a sound that invokes the Presence and a sound that provokes the Lord; it's time we discern the difference. We should expect that the Holy Spirit will dictate the direction of the ministry on any given day through sensitive leadership. We should expect to see manifestation of the intangible in our midst. Most of all, we must prepare ourselves to be in the Presence like this generation has never known or understood. This will be frightening to some, and others will quickly embrace it. Yet I believe that what we will experience will far exceed the glorious day of past historical revival-type events that we have recently tried to resurrect. We must examine the passages that reveal the Father's glory in that it was, for lack of a better term, *spectacular!*

No longer will this generation be content with "having church" or departing from a service and rendering it as a "good service."

Those terms will no longer be adequate to describe "entering into the presence of the Almighty." I am looking for Most Holy Place experiences only. In these times, as in the days of Solomon, we will fall down prostrate in the cloud of His presence. Or as in the case of Moses, we will realize the place we stand is holy. Or we will be like Ezekiel, who fell on his face when the glory of the Lord returned to the temple. These days are far removed from us. This generation has never known them. They only know the dazzling splash of colored lights and video displays with the leaders who have mastered the profession of religious entertainment in the name of the Lord. So the remnant who can recall (even slightly) the days of humility and dependence on the Holy Spirit in worship will have to stand alone and declare that the tabernacle of David is about to be restored!

CHAPTER 12

THE FUTURE OF WORSHIP

So what does this all mean? If you receive what is written in this book, what will worship look like in the future? Here, I will go over some key points and highlight what the Lord has revealed to me that initiated this process and brought me to this place.

What was most obvious to me was that, as a pastor, I was beginning to experience the boredom of a traditional worship service. An acknowledgment of this reality was a necessary launching pad for change. I was unconvinced that these old systems based on antiquated revelation were still valid and applicable in this era of the Church; this helped to foster drastic changes. With this in my spirit, I was able to open myself up to things I was unfamiliar with in worship and things that were yet to be revealed.

Reconnecting my faith and theology to my Jewish roots came as a Holy Spirit-orchestrated second step. Instead of walking away from my leadership position after three years of pastoring and returning to my evangelical ministry of the previous twelve years, I walked into an interaction with a Jewish believer whose words still ring in my memory to this day. He came to The Worship Center (which at that time was still Christ's Gospel Baptist Church) on a cold Wednesday night in January 2002. Because of the weather, there were fewer than twenty people present, and I felt like his coming was a waste of his time.

He sat in my little office and calmly stated, "What if I'm not here for them; what if I'm here for you?" Then after a short conversation, I immediately knew that three quarters of my Gentile theology would have to be dramatically modified or discarded, and I was very excited about the new information that I was about to receive. This launched my quest to understand, from a Hebraic perspective, the faith that I had received as an eight-year-old boy. This is also a necessary component for embracing much of the perspectives that I have outlined in this book. And it is important to note that this became, for me, a seven-year journey.

I should also note that this journey began simultaneously with our divorce from the Baptist denominational affiliation. These changes taking place at the same time put my ministry and my pastoral leadership at great risk. My critics were many and vocal. The already small congregation shrunk in size to about twenty-five people. The church finances dwindled to the point that we functioned in the red for three years. Without the savings we had accumulated over the previous three years, we would not have survived.

Throughout the entire time, I held on to what was being revealed and preached, and I taught it almost without regard for the repercussions. Ninety percent of those who began the journey with me left at that point. There was a temptation to return to my career on Wall Street or at least ramp up my evangelism ministry for personal recognition and financial support. Neither of those happened. I remained resolute that G-d had favored me with some amazing revelations and that they would bless the Body of Christ in a dramatic way if I just remained committed to the process. More than ten years later, I'm glad I never wavered.

Viewing the Scriptures from a Hebraic perspective opened up things in the Bible I could not see before with my Gentile denominational glasses on. I began to rehash the main events of Old Testament worship and understand that this picture has application in my modern faith. Now I needed the help of the Holy Spirit to appreciate how to connect it and apply it to my worship today. This journey took us through major Bible studies on the Ten Commandments and the Ark of the Covenant, both of which prepared us for the study called "From Tabernacle to Temple, Synagogue to Sanctuary," from which this book is written.

What followed were extraordinary corporate worship experiences at TWC. We saw supernatural manifestations of His Presence followed by healing, deliverance, and revelations of the kingdom. G-d began to do things in our midst that were simply mesmerizing. At the same time, we began to take the emphasis off of the trendy hot topics of that day such as prosperity, church growth, seeker-friendly services, technology and marketing, church hierarchy (choir leaders and singers being elevated to pastors, pastors being elevated to bishops, and so forth), and networking. We did strange things like rip up the program and throw it away. We ceased to receive offerings by appeal and passing the plate. The congregation began to bring it during worship and praise without coercion or manipulation. We began to honor the Sabbath the way the Scripture says and give the whole day to worship, rest, and family time. People began to linger around the church facility long after the service was over. In general, we avoid planning or scheduling anything on the Sabbath other than worship. We also began celebrating the three feasts that the Scripture says should never cease: Passover, Firstfruits, and Ingathering. With the inclusion of these biblical celebrations, we were able to depart from traditional celebrations like anniversaries, pastor appreciation, auxiliary celebrations, and all those other days we've created just to keep people busy.

What was noticed immediately was that the environment became less competitive. The leadership wasn't competing with other leaders, and the congregation had less infighting. We began to recognize that we are one Body in Christ in truth and we have a diversity of gifts that are authorized by the same Spirit. We honor the work of the janitor in the same way we honor the gift in the apostle. We began to sense a spirit of unity and family among the saints, and it still exists to this day.

One of the most notable things that has happened over the last few years is the transition of the music ministry. "The Levites," as they are comfortably referred to at TWC, have taken on the responsibility of singing and making melody before the Lord and not the people. In doing this, they help to provide an atmosphere that is irresistible to the presence of the Almighty. This is no longer done with popular songs heard on the radio, since we don't know how those songs were birthed. Our Levitical pastor, myself, and some others now write the songs and compose the music that we believe epitomizes what the Lord is doing at TWC and what is pleasing to Him in sound and words. These songs have transformed the worship.

Sometimes a song will be sung for twenty minutes just because the Holy Spirit is using it to minister to the Father or to bring us closer to the kingdom. In this, we know that we are not presenting strange fire and subjecting ourselves to removal from His Presence. This alone is sometimes the joy of worshiping at TWC—just hearing a song that we know He gave us for His glory. (Many of these songs should be available now for the Body of Christ to embrace.) We have no choirs competing with one another, just dedicated Levites who tirelessly minister before the Lord every Sunday. They have no pre-scripted format. They are in no rush to get to the next thing. They simply sing before the Lord with all of their hearts (sometimes for an hour and a half), with a mindset that they are to please Him in song, not the people. It is wonderful to have this type of spontaneous worship experience every Sunday.

I passively mentioned how the offerings are received previously, but I should elaborate on it briefly. Since one of the things that is ruining ministry today is the aggressive solicitation of money, I had to ask the Lord to give us a way to receive the offerings without the manipulation and coercion. It was during this Bible study that the Lord spoke to us a very specific word right in the midst of the class.

At the time, we were dealing with the introduction of the tabernacle in the days of Moses. YHWH spoke to Moses and told him to have the people build a sanctuary so that He could dwell among them (see Exod. 25:8). As I studied the process of preparation for the tabernacle, I noticed in Exodus 36 that the people brought "freewill" offerings continually until there were more than enough resources to complete the tabernacle. In fact, Moses issued a command that they should cease to bring offerings for the tabernacle in verse 6. When I saw this, I said to the Lord, "Why don't we have this problem today?" Essentially, we never get to the place where the leader stops the people from bringing money for anything.

So the Lord brought me back to Exodus 25:8 and showed me why they brought the money freely the way they did. It was for one reason; they had the guarantee that He would dwell among them. The motivation for their giving was not the tabernacle; the tabernacle was the thing the offerings were used for, and they were honored to be participants in the creation of this new concept and structure. The motivation was that YHWH would dwell among them; that's all. It was upon this revelation that we stopped passing offering plates and making offering appeals. Other than teaching members about tithing in new members/converts class, there is very little mention of it. Instead, we have shifted to bringing our tithes freely and willingly. Not only that, but the motivation for giving is never a project or a need; it is always, "Give if you believe the presence of YHWH is here, and give to secure that His presence will remain."

When offerings are received, we have the opportunity to insure the Lord's presence in our midst. Once we made that shift, the people began to feel the release to give willingly out of their hearts. For the first few weeks, like with anything, people were apprehensive and maybe even confused. However, after about a month, the offerings began to increase five to ten percent and have not stopped increasing since, even during the recent recession. This was very risky because typically, when we don't appeal for money, it doesn't manifest. This was quite different; we depend on the presence of the Lord to do the work that we the leaders can't do, even if we tried. He convicts the hearts and challenges our practices. One other thing should be noted; we only receive the Lord's offering once a week!

In this age of corrupt and greedy church leadership, the Lord has privileged us to raise enough money to do ministry locally and in some fifteen countries, including buying Bibles and building churches in Myanmar and Thailand, supporting an orphanage and a church in India, supporting two students in college in Zambia, supporting a church building project in South Africa, and most recently, partnering to launch a micro-financing work in Haiti, just to name a few. In all of these projects, we never have to raise a "special offering" to accomplish these projects. At the same time, we have seen supernatural financial manifestations in the lives of many in TWC.

Another very important facet of worship in the future will be the internal structure of the ministry. Most ministries today are built upon one or two super-dynamic personalities. These personalities are primarily credited with drawing the people into that church from week to week. In most cases, if you remove the driving forces of any large ministry and replace them with people who are less charismatic, the ministry will dwindle in a short period of time. This is indicative of the structure that the ministry is built upon. Yet the truth is that in many cases these personalities are commanding the type of attention that only the Head of the Church should invoke.

Worship in the future will have a tangible multi-personality leadership model. Though we have for the most part relegated the leadership of a church to one pastor, this model is probably not the best for that person or the followers. There really needs to be a plurality of pastors, teachers, and evangelists who have authoritative responsibility in the congregation. Then, as Paul mentions at least three times specifically in his letters, the apostles and prophets serve foundationally in the Church. The empowerment of many leaders to walk in their giftings keeps one or two people from subtly being worshiped by the masses. This dramatic but necessary change allows for a different type of worship to emerge in the sanctuary. It might begin as a psychological shift, but it will end up being that a congregation gradually moves away from personality-driven worship.

The change I believe will be most difficult to embrace and implement will be the design of the sanctuary. Most will write this off as being Old Testament and non-applicable. Others have said to me that the saint is the temple of the Holy Spirit, and therefore, the building design does not impact the New Testament Church experience. Yet I emphasize that my approach to this subject is birthed out of the historical facts that prove that our present sanctuary concept is purely and undeniably Roman. It has no scriptural basis or precedent, and until there are facts that suggest that G-d abandoned His design (for His house) for a Roman design, I cannot agree.

In all of Scripture, there is but one pattern given to people (by YHWH) for the design of His sanctuary. The pattern remained consistent throughout Scripture and was never scripturally abandoned. The design mimics the temple in Heaven (see Rev. 11:18), even down to the presence of the Ark. What we have done in the Gentile Church is come up with our own designs, which in fact speak to what we deem preeminent in these designs. Thus, we glorify the person in the pulpit (or behind the podium or on the director's chair) by virtue of the design and pattern that we use. What I scripturally advocate is that we make YHWH preeminent by giving Him His proper and prominent space in the sanctuary. The only way I know to do that is by providing a Most Holy Place with the Ark and the cherubim.

Now I am very aware of the theological and natural challenge that this creates. However, I am more in tune with the results that we will see in corporate worship as a result of giving YHWH His proper place in our midst. No longer will He share His glory with some person whom we have typically celebrated. He will share His glory with no one, and all of us will fall at His feet and bow our heads in humility and gratitude that we have audience with the King of the universe. The need and the time for this type of corporate worship experience is now. We cannot afford to wallow around in the muddy waters of ineffective worship. The atmosphere is right for a return to what David set forth with his little tent. The Church is in desperate need of a glorious experience that is not orchestrated by the flesh. YHWH's desire is stronger than ever to refresh and rekindle the fires of the soul that have gone out. He waits expectantly to expose His extraordinary presence to worshipers who come before Him, abandoning their agendas. He will overwhelm the churches with an atmosphere full of His glory, and we will be satisfied with Him alone. I'm sure by now that you are anticipating and hungering after this type of experience every time you walk into the Lord's sanctuary. When you enter His house, you will expect to experience His glory!

The restoration of the Most Holy Place will be the most dramatic and controversial move the modern Church will make (or deny). In it we will see the difference, but not because we have started a new trend or movement; the difference will be in the powerful and overwhelming demonstration of the Presence of YHWH. That will be the only proof that we have only proof that we have done the right thing and that the Father is pleased.

The structures that exist today for the use of worship will eventually be seen as non-biblical by origin. What has fascinated me throughout the development of this revelation is that YHWH never said to build a sanctuary for the amount of people in Israel at that time, as we do today. We build for all the wrong reasons and expect

G-d to bless it and provide for it. Unfortunately, when most churches are celebrating a new building, in reality most are celebrating a mortgage and the earmarking of future offerings. The one who's really celebrating is the bank who loaned them the money!

As we prepare to eliminate the things that have been brought into "the worship of the Lord" that should have never been there, we should expect to see the ministry of the Holy Spirit return to the Church in a mighty way. In Matthew 21:13-14, Jesus entered the temple and expelled everyone and everything that did not represent the Father's original intent for His house. John 2:17 says of Jesus, "... *Zeal for Your house has eaten Me up"*; this is the way we must feel about Father's house. Nothing unauthorized shall enter and taint the atmosphere. Nothing will diminish the glory and power of His Presence. Nothing shall disturb and distract from giving our attention to Adonai. We must aggressively expel the practices, structures, hierarchies, idols, images, religious liturgies, human-made boundaries, and limitations that have so weakened the perception of the most powerful community in the world: the Body of Christ.

It was only after Jesus expelled the religious foolishness in Matthew 21:14 that the authentic work of the Holy Spirit returned. The Bible says that the blind and the lame came to the same temple and that the Holy Spirit began to heal and deliver them through Christ. This is amazing. In the same location where the leadership was preoccupied with doing things their own way, after they and their practices were removed, people began to flock in for real ministry. If we would only be willing to depart from the foolishness we have labeled "church" and move into the authentic that the Father has labeled "worship," we would experience His Presence, see the broken and disillusioned come flocking in, and see the Holy Spirit deliver them.

In the future of worship, we will see pastors and leaders immersed in and driven by a desire to be in the Presence. This will in turn create a people whose only motivation for coming to worship is the Presence of the Lord. When we enter into His house, we will get a real sense that we are, in fact, in a unique and sanctified place in the city. The freedom that will be experienced will be impossible to duplicate. The sanctuary will be defined by His glory. What the Earth longs for is the revealing of the sons of G-d. This exposure will be directly related to those who spend time in His presence in the sanctuary. The kingdom of G-d will take on significance in every area of the saint's life. There will be an authenticity that sets believers apart and distinguishes them when they are out in the marketplace doing their daily tasks.

Christians everywhere are hungry for the type of experience that John experienced on the Isle of Patmos. We have assumed that these things were only for that season; however, a careful look at Scripture suggests that this is far from the truth. In fact, the emphatic ripping of the veil from "top to bottom" and the exposure of the Most Holy Place could only mean that YHWH's eternal desire to be with His people has never dissipated. Matthew 27:51-52 makes it very clear that the Father was demonstrating earthshaking changes in the way worship would be experienced now that His presence was being exposed openly again. Not only would the Earth recognize His glory, but even the dead would be called back to life. Isn't this what the gospel and the kingdom represent? People who were dead in trespasses and sins are, via an earthshaking experience called the death of Jesus Christ, now reunited in glorious fellowship with the Father. Now all of those who long to walk with G-d in the cool of the day as Adam did will have that chance.

In the future, worship will look just like that—walking with G-d, experiencing His presence, enjoying His house, seeing His glory, and inviting others into that glorious environment. His house will be a refuge, a fortress, a high-tower, a pavilion that all will long to be hidden inside of. David could not have said it better in Psalm 27:4,

One thing have I desired of the Lord, that will I seek after;
that I may dwell in the house of the Lord all the days of my
life, to behold the beauty of the Lord, and to enquire in his
temple (KJV).

There has been a cataclysmic shaking in the spirit realm; there is a tsunami wave of change headed toward the Body of Christ, and only those who have instinctively discerned the times will be prepared for what is to come. I hope this has helped you to prepare.

Shalom.

ABOUT NATHAN BYRD

For more information about Jesus Makes the Difference Ministries or Nathan Byrd, please contact Valerie Riddick at:

914-606-0393.

IN THE RIGHT HANDS, THIS BOOK WILL CHANGE LIVES!

Most of the people who need this message will not be looking for this book. To change their lives, you need to put a copy of this book in their hands.

> *But others (seeds) fell into good ground, and brought forth fruit, some a hundred-fold, some sixty-fold, some thirty-fold* (Matthew 13:8).

Our ministry is constantly seeking methods to find the good ground, the people who need this anointed message to change their lives. Will you help us reach these people?

> *Remember this—a farmer who plants only a few seeds will get a small crop. But the one who plants generously will get a generous crop* (2 Corinthians 9:6).

EXTEND THIS MINISTRY BY SOWING
3 BOOKS, 5 BOOKS, 10 BOOKS, OR MORE TODAY,
AND BECOME A LIFE CHANGER!

Thank you,

Don Nori Sr., Founder
Destiny Image
Since 1982